Islam and Its Festivals

Istafiah Is'harc

TA-HA Publishers
1 Wynne Road
London SW9 0BB
U.K.

Copyright © Ta-Ha Publishers Ltd. 1997

Published in Rabiᶜ ath-Thani 1418 AH/August 1997 CE by

Ta-Ha Publishers Ltd.
1 Wynne Road
London SW9 0BB
website:http://www.taha.co.uk/
email: sale@taha.co.uk

By: Istafiah Is'harc
Edited by: ᶜAbdassamad Clarke

British Library Cataloguing in Publication Data
Islam and Its Festivals
1. Is'harc, Istafiah

ISBN 1 897940 67 X

Typeset by: ᶜAbdassamad Clarke.

Printed and Bound by- De-Luxe Printers,
London NW10 7NR.
website: http://www.de-luxe.com
email: naresh@aapi.co.uk

Contents

Acknowledgements

I would like express my thanks to Dr. Latimah Peerwani who gave me much encouragement and invaluable advice on an earlier draft of this book especially with regard to historical accuracy. My thanks also to Mrs. H. Halim of the Iqra Trust, London for her help and information on the Hajj. I am grateful for the sensitive and professional editorial advice given to me so generously by Lawrence Brazier, who has the advantage of drawing on many years experience as a writer. I would also like to express my thanks and appreciation to Dr. Aliya Hajji who looked over my work with a critical and learned eye and was able to make many helpful suggestions. Above all I would like to thank my family for their enthusiasm and support for this book – especially my beloved husband who was able to provide me with insights into the experience of the Hajj and other facets of the story of Islam. There are many others who have in various ways – and sometimes quite unknowingly – contributed to this book, to whom I would like to extend my gratitude as well, especially the hajjis whom I have had the good fortune to meet and whose accounts of their experiences have touched me deeply.

Part One: Islam

CHAPTER ONE: ABOUT ISLAM

Thirteen hundred years ago an event took place in the Middle East, the results of which we can still feel to this day in almost every part of the world. Ripple-like, its effects moved both East and West, and it was especially during the Dark and Middle Ages in Europe that the developments arising from this event began to touch the lives of people. A new and inspiring force, it brought change, enlightenment and creativity which affected the lives, the thinking and the culture of millions.

This event was the birth of an extraordinary man – a man of noble lineage who was born into humble circumstances. During his life as a young child, he experienced tragedy – the deaths of his mother and two years later, his grandfather – his father having died before his birth. Although he was well loved by his uncle and other relatives, he understood well the loneliness of being an orphan. He grew up to be a man with a reputation for honesty and trustworthiness, and became a trader traversing the deserts of Arabia. In due course, he married a wealthy widow – a woman who was older than him but who was highly respected in Makkan society. She was also a very beautiful, compassionate person with strong principles and beliefs. Then something happened to dramatically alter his life and it was this which was also the beginning of this tremendous force for change. A devoted and spiritual man, he had withdrawn to a cave to fast and pray when one night he was visited by the Angel Jibril (Gabriel) who proclaimed to him his true vocation in life. This man who was called 'Muhammad' ﷺ was commanded by Allah to become His Prophet and Messenger. So began a battle to reinstate high social and spiritual values, to destroy idolatry and replace it with a way of life based on the worship of Allah, the One, the Almighty God, a way which is called Islam. It is a story in which this honest man of humble origins, guided by Allah, proved to have qualities, character, intelligence and skills unsurpassed by any human being either before or since that time. It is a story of great faith and courage, a tale of the miraculous as well as the commonplace.

Today, Islam is one of the great world religions with some 1,300 million followers in countries as far apart as Arabia, the United States of America, Great Britain, South Africa, China and Australia. It has its roots in the time of the Prophet Ibrahim, peace be upon him, and Judaism and Christianity are two deviant offshoots from the great central trunk of Islam. The prophets of Islam are also those who are recognised by the Jewish and Christian Books, although the Old Testament contains much defamation of their characters and the New Testament – flying to the opposite extreme – idolisation of 'Isa, peace be upon him and upon them all, so that the Qur'an uniquely restores their honour from both slander and idolatry.

The Prophet Muhammad ﷺ a descendant of the prophets Ibrahim and Isma'il, 'alaihima's-salam, was born in Makkah in about 570 CE. Growing up in a society in which most people had forgotten Allah and worshipped idols instead, the Prophet Muhammad ﷺ was chosen by Allah to remind people of the Oneness of Allah and to turn them away from idol-worship. During his twenty-three years of prophethood, the Prophet and Messenger of Allah Muhammad ﷺ brought immense and important changes to the Arab people. They mostly comprised warring tribes which the Prophet succeeded in uniting through the grace of Allah in Islam. His influence reached beyond religious belief to areas such as health, education, and the establishment and administration of a governance founded on justice and compassion. After his death, Islam continued to spread through the world and just a hundred years later, Muslim rule stretched East to the Himalayas and West as far as Gibraltar and almost up to the Pyrenees (indeed areas of France such as Narbonne were Muslim amirates for more than thirty years). At a time when Europe was in the Dark Ages, Islam flourished and brought a civilising influence to the borders of the Europeans. It played an important role in world history, and you can still see the influence of Islamic art, science and philosophy in much of western and world culture today.

Examples of Islamic influence in the world and especially in Europe can be found in our numerals which are taken from Arabic numerals. The Arabs based their system of numbers on the

Indian numerals and developed them further. When they invented the 'zero', it became possible to do the complicated calculations which were so essential for the development of astronomy and many other branches of science such as physics. Previously, Roman numerals had been used in the West, and these were much clumsier to work with. Many of the words we use today such as algebra, sugar, saffron, syrup, arsenal, alkali, antimony, nadir and zenith also come from the Arabic. The Muslims became great mathematicians and astronomers and developed the compass. Medicine was another field in which they made great strides breaking into completely new areas – especially in the study of infectious diseases, opthalmology and herbal remedies. By about the tenth century, they were able to name all the bones, muscles and veins of the body.

Other things that they brought the West were: glass in the form of mirrors as well as stained-glass, melons, apricots, coffee, ginger, onions, lemons, the violin, chess, techniques for irrigation and even windmills.

The word Islam derives from a root meaning peace and means surrender or the submission of a person's will to obedience to Allah and His Messenger and to those in authority among the Muslims. The way of Islam is not only a teaching to show people how to pray and worship Allah, but it is also a guidance for us in how to live our lives. It is a complete way of life. This guidance is found mainly in the Noble Qur'an and in the Sunnah of the Messenger of Allah ﷺ and of the Khalifahs after him who took the right way.

The Glorious Qur'an is the book which contains all the verbal revelations the Prophet Muhammad ﷺ received from Allah. It is in a beautiful and exquisite Arabic form which is yet not poetry and indeed far exalted above poetry, and many Muslims read, recite or chant it daily. The Qur'an is an inspiring book which contains stories about the prophets, good advice for people and examples for their lives. It shows what can happen to people when they live in an evil way, and also tells of the joy people can experience when they worship Allah and the rewards promised to those who remember the Almighty all through their lives, do good deeds and look after the weak and needy. It is not permitted to ever change the words of the Noble Qur'an, and indeed it is an impossibility since Allah has guaranteed in one of its ayat to guard and preserve it.

Muslims can also find guidance for their lives in the Sunnah. This is practice of the Prophet ☙ and of his khalifahs.

A MUSLIM BELIEVES IN THREE BASIC THINGS:

Tawhid: Belief that Allah is One – He has no parents, no partners and no children. He alone is the Creator and He alone should be worshipped.

Risalah: That belief in the Prophets and Messengers of Allah which is exemplified by living in obedience to them. Since human beings were first created on this earth, Allah has sent His prophets and messengers to the world to guide men and women. They taught people how to live their lives according to the command of Allah, and to love and worship Him. When people went astray, Allah would send another prophet. There are different understandings of what is the difference between a prophet and a messenger, the most famous of which is that a Prophet receives revelation from Allah but is not necessarily commanded to convey it to people, whereas a messenger is commanded to summon people to belief and obedience. Three of the messengers before Islam – Musa, Dawud and 'Isa ☙ – are believed to have received revealed books, although the books of the Christians and the Jews today are probably no longer the same as those revelations. The Prophet Muhammad ☙ is the Last Prophet and the Glorious Qur'an is the last revealed Book. The Messenger of Allah ☙ was given a special barakah – grace or blessing – by Allah, glorious is He and exalted, which he was able to transmit along with the prayers and practices of Islam. Many find that they feel and experience this barakah by reading the Noble Qur'an and trying to live as the Prophet ☙ commanded and advised them to. In this age when Islam no longer truly exists as a fully functioning society this requires no uncommon courage and struggle to bring about the full Muslim Ummah again with the implementation of the shari'ah in obedience to a Khalifah or successor of the Messenger of Allah ☙.

Akhirah: Belief in the Day of Judgement and life after death.

Two angels keep a record of each person's deeds, and on the Day of Judgement these records will be shown to that person in the presence of Allah. A person who has worshipped Allah alone, sincerely without associating anything with Him and done good deeds during his lifetime, will be rewarded with the joys of Paradise (Jannah). If a person has turned away from Allah and lived a bad life, his punishment will be the terrible fires of Hell (Jahannam).

MUSLIM NOT MUHAMMADAN

People who live in Islam are not called Muhammadans, but Muslims. The meaning of the word Muslim is a person who submits to the law of Allah and to the Sunnah. Islam is regarded as the way of Allah, not the religion of Muhammad. Muslims see the Prophet Muhammad ﷺ as a special person chosen by Allah to be His Messenger. However, they do not worship him. Muhammad came to renew the way of the Prophet Ibrahim (Abraham) ﷺ , the Way of Allah. He did not invent a new religion. For these reasons, it is not correct to call a Muslim a Muhammadan.

THE LAND OF MAKKAH

Makkah, the city where the Prophet Muhammad ﷺ was born, lies in the Hijaz Peninsula of the area we call Arabia (Saudi is the family name of the present dynasty). It is situated in a dry and arid part of the world which especially today more than ever is nearly all desert, since the deserts of the world are expanding. The only green areas were the few oases where caravans would stop on their long journeys across the desert. There were sometimes large settlements around the oases where dates and other crops such as wheat were grown. Travellers stopped there for rest and shade for themselves and their camels. Most of all, they stopped for water and to stock up with food for the journey.

Today the climate remains unchanged and the sun is burning hot during the hours of daylight. The desert nights can be cool – sometimes bitterly cold – while overhead the inky night sky throbs with the light of the twinkling stars. From time to time there might be a sandstorm, when the strong winds raise moving clouds of sand which whip and attack man and beast with a very great force. There is no escape from a sandstorm if you are in the middle of the desert. The only thing you can do is to lie down flat, covering yourself as best as you can, until it has passed. Occasionally, there might be a big storm with heavy rain, and this sometimes causes bad flooding in the valleys. Arabia is a land of stark contrasts.

THE TIMES OF THE PROPHET MUHAMMAD ﷺ

Muhammad ﷺ was born into a society which comprised various tribes – many nomadic and some very powerful. Over the centuries, some of the tribes had settled in Makkah. The tribe of Quraysh, to which the Prophet ﷺ belonged, had already lived there since the time of Isma'il ﷺ . Makkah became a thriving city. Money became of very great importance and people forgot many of their old values. In the desert, life could sometimes be brutal and violent. Wars frequently occurred between the tribes, and although the fatalities were often incredibly few compared to the wars we have seen in our times, there was sometimes little respect for other human beings.

It could be even worse if you were a female because women had a very low and insecure position in society. Men would sometimes gamble away their wives as if they were just a bit of property and not human beings at all. At that time it was not unusual for baby girls to be buried alive. Prisoners taken during battles often became slaves, and they too were frequently very badly treated.

However, these tribes also had ancient customs and ways. Some of them made agreements with their neighbours to keep the peace and prevent the battles that killed off so many of the men. They did not like to break these agreements. Honour was also very important to the Arabs. If one of their own people was killed, they would have to avenge the person's death. When the killing might have been an accident, the victim's tribe might sometimes agree to accept 'blood money' as compensation.

The tribes had developed their own pagan religions and worshipped many idols. The Ka'bah in Makkah, was the very first temple to Allah – the One God – built thousands of years ago by the Prophet Ibrahim and his son Isma'il, 'alaihima's-salam.

The Black Stone – which is said to have been a meteorite – is located on an outside corner of the structure. It is said to be the first stone to fall to earth as a sign of the covenant between Allah and human beings, and some believe that the Angel Jibril brought it from Heaven. Through the centuries, most of the Quraysh forgot the religion of their forefather, the Prophet Ibrahim ~~~ . They had become pagans and no longer worshipped Allah – the One God – but worshipped idols instead. By the time the Messenger of Allah ~~~ was born, the Ka'bah housed 360 idols. It had become a major centre for idol worship.

Apart from the Arabs who had their own religions, there were also some settlements of Jews and a few Christians living in that area.

HOW SOCIETY CHANGED AS A RESULT OF THE PROPHET MUHAMMAD'S TEACHINGS

The Prophet Muhammad ~~~ had many revelations from Allah through which he was commanded that he should bring people back to worship Allah, the One God. He taught the Arabs how to live in a better way. Following divine guidance he established, first by his own absolute obedience to the revelation and by his extraordinary generosity, the shari'ah and the sunnah which ensure that the old, the poor, children, orphans and slaves are cared for.

There were revelations specifically to help women. Men have to protect and be gentle and kind to women. Women can no longer be forced to marry someone they do not like. When a couple marry, the bride is to be given a dowry by the bridegroom which she has agreed with the help of her guardian. The money, jewels or property that she is given are her own, and she can use them in any way that she wants. Possibly as a result of battles, there were many more women than men in Arab society. The Qur'an, allows a man to take up to four wives – but only if he treats them all equally! By also encouraging the men to marry widows, orphaned children are given the protection of their new stepfathers. The Prophet ~~~ was always concerned that women should be protected.

Many of the Muslim women including the Prophet's wives,

went out on to the battlefields to help the wounded, and a few even played a part in the fighting. Although the Prophet ﷺ discouraged women from participating in the battles, he did not stop them. A woman called Umm Ammarah, was once seriously wounded while defending the Prophet ﷺ. It is interesting that at the time the Messenger of Allah ﷺ was improving women's rights in Arabia, far away in France, a council of Christian bishops met to discuss whether women had souls!

The Prophet ﷺ put a very high value on education and learning. He himself did not read. This was part of his greatest miracle for since he neither read nor had studied with anyone and in view of the tremendous knowledge and wisdom he had and the miraculous nature of the Qur'an, it was clear that Allah revealed to him and taught him. In fact, at that time, very few people were able to read. When he married A'ishah she was still very young, and he insisted that she learn to read and write. She was a very intelligent and learned woman, and after the Prophet's death, many people used to come to her to ask her for guidance on the practice and wisdom of Islam.

Although the Prophet ﷺ was a kind and compassionate man, he sometimes had to make difficult decisions and punish people for their crimes. Allah also gave His guidance to the Prophet ﷺ as to how people should be punished. Because society was so wild and lawless then – and is even more so today, if one reads the newspapers – the punishments are heavy. For example, if a person is caught stealing he has his right hand cut off. Although this may seem a terrible punishment, it is fair. In England as late as 1820, people would be hanged for stealing when they were only stealing from starvation. In the shari'ah it is forbidden to punish people who steal because of desperate hunger.

The Prophet Muhammad ﷺ followed the guidance he received from Allah, and laid the foundations for a society that is just and fair. It is a society in which people take care of each other. The community he developed is called the Ummah in Arabic. Today, although the Ummah is still a very important part of a Muslim's life, it technically speaking does not exist since Islam is no longer embodied as a social reality, there is no khalifah and no rulers who govern by the Shari'ah and the zakat is not collected and distributed. To be a Muslim today means a dynamic effort to recreate all of that which our Muslim forbears took for granted.

Many people found the Prophet's ideas revolutionary because he wanted to give the weak protection and all people fair opportunities. As a result, the idol worshippers felt threatened by the new teaching. The Quraysh were also afraid that the gods they worshipped would be angry with them if they began to worship Allah alone, the 'One God'. There was another reason as to why they were unhappy with the religion that the Prophet ﷺ was spreading. The Ka'bah and the many idols it housed, was a place of pilgrimage for people from a very wide area. These pilgrims brought wealth to the city. If suddenly instead of 360 gods there was only one God who did not live only in Makkah but existed everywhere, the Quraysh were liable to lose a lot of money!

THE MUSLIM CALENDAR

The Muslim calendar starts from the year of the Hijrah which was in 622 AD. This was the year when the Muslims of Makkah emigrated to Madinah. The Muslim calendar is ten days shorter than the Gregorian Calendar (eleven days shorter in a leap year) because it is based on lunar months. The Gregorian Calendar, a solar calendar derived from the calendar of the old sun-worshipping Roman Empire, is used in most countries in the world today because of the dominance of western Christianity which extended the life of the old Roman Empire. The lunar calendar is the original calendar of mankind, for even the English word 'month' derives from moon, and the period of a month of around 30-31 days is approximately the period of the moon's cycle which is twenty-nine and a half days. The new moon marks the first day of each lunar month. The lunar calendar was used in the ancient world because, like most of the earth's peoples throughout history, they were people of the fitrah and most of them could not read. It is easy for anyone to see the new moon, and in this way to know when the new month is beginning. Any other system will always need a priesthood, even if a mathematical priesthood, and "there is no priesthood in Islam". The importance of this in Islam will become clear later.

Chapter 2: The Prophet Muhammad in Makkah

THE PROPHET MUHAMMAD'S CHILDHOOD

When Aminah, the Prophet Muhammad's mother became pregnant she knew that her baby must be someone special because she often saw light emanating from her womb. On one occasion she saw this light flash and illuminate all the way to Syria. On another occasion she had a vision in which she heard a voice which told her that she was carrying the 'Prince of this nation'. She was also told that when he was born he was to be put 'under the protection of the only One (Allah)' and was to be named 'Muhammad'. She was known to remark that she never experienced any of the discomfort that women sometimes experience during pregnancy nor did she ever feel that she was carrying any weight. Abdullah, the baby's father was known for his fine features, radiance of his expression and his excellent character. Sadly, he died before his son's birth. So when Muhammad ﷺ was born, Aminah called for the baby's grandfather, 'Abd al-Muttalib. When she told him about her vision, he immediately took the baby to the Ka'bah to pray to Allah and to offer thanks for His gift.

The climate in Makkah was considered unhealthy – especially for young children – and because of this, the Makkans had a custom of giving their babies to be looked after by a wet-nurse from another tribe from the desert. The wet-nurses were usually from Bedouin tribes living in a greener and healthier area. They looked after the infants for a number of years and would return to Makkah from time to time so that the children could see their parents.

One day, a woman called Halimah was travelling to Makkah with her husband and baby, and some of her tribe. These women were looking for infants to suckle. Times were difficult – Halimah's she-camel and sheep were not producing any milk. The family was close to starvation and her baby cried all night from hunger. Even their donkey was so weak that it lagged behind the others, and Halimah's tribes-people would constantly chide her and call the family to catch up with them. When at last, they arrived in Makkah, none of the other women wanted to take the baby Muhammad ﷺ because he was an orphan. The women were all hoping to secure good connections for themselves and their children with the babies' fathers for looking after their babies – and Muhammad ﷺ had no father. Halimah's friends soon found infants and were impatient to return home. Not wishing to return without a baby, Halimah decided to take the orphan.

Then amazing things started to happen. As she went to feed the baby Muhammad ﷺ, she felt her breasts fill with milk and after feeding him there was more than enough milk for her own baby son. The she-camel also produced so much milk that Halimah and her husband were able to drink their fill. Their donkey started trotting so fast that the others could not keep up with them. When they returned home – despite the difficult times – their sheep too, began to produce milk in abundance. Their neighbours were very surprised and could not understand what had happened. They thought that the grass where Halimah's sheep grazed was better than where their sheep were being pastured. So they moved their sheep to graze with Halimah's, but the sheep still did not produce any more milk than they had done before. Halimah and her husband soon realised that the baby in their care was someone very special.

There are many other amazing stories about the Prophet Muhammad ﷺ which all show that he was an extraordinary person, and was blessed with grace by Allah.

When he was only six years old his mother died, so he went to live with his grandfather, 'Abd al-Muttalib who doted on his grandson. Two years later his dying grandfather entrusted the young child to his uncle, Abu Talib. In a period of just two years, little Muhammad ﷺ had experienced the loss of the two people who had loved him greatly. His life was about to change again. While Muhammad ﷺ had lived with Halimah, he had helped to herd sheep, but now not wishing to be left behind at home, he accompanied his uncle on a long journey to trade in Syria.

On this journey Bahira, a monk, saw Muhammad ﷺ. He had known for a long time that there was going to be another prophet and when he saw the young Muhammad ﷺ, he could tell by various signs that this boy was without doubt the prophet that people were waiting for. He warned Abu Talib to take great care of him.

MUHAMMAD THE YOUNG MAN

As Muhammad ﷺ grew up he rejected the idols that people worshipped at that time. He turned only to Allah, the One. Muhammad ﷺ gained a high reputation among his people, the Quraysh tribe, who called him Al-Amin – the Trustworthy. They called on him to settle their disputes, because they knew that he was always fair and just. They also gave him their goods to look after.

When he was about twenty-five years old Muhammad ﷺ started working for Khadijah ﵂ a wealthy and highly respected woman of the same tribe. Khadijah employed him to take merchandise to sell in Syria. When he returned she was delighted that he had traded so successfully, especially when she sold the goods he brought back at an excellent profit. But more than that, she heard stories about him from her slave, Maysara, who had accompanied him on this journey. Maysara told Khadijah that a monk in Syria called Nestor, had recognised his master as the prophet that people had been waiting for. He also said that when they were crossing the desert during the hottest part of the day, he had himself seen two angels with spread wings, protecting Muhammad ﷺ from the midday sun.

Khadijah ﵂ was a widow, and she was also older than Muhammad. Despite this she was still very attractive and many men had asked her to marry them, but she had always refused. However, she liked Muhammad's qualities and felt drawn to him by his honourable and truthful character, and decided to ask him to marry her and he accepted. They grew to love each other very deeply, and through some very difficult times Khadijah ﵂ remained a very loyal and devoted wife. Although she was wealthy and of a noble class, she seemed to understand how it felt to be poor. She used all her wealth to help Muhammad ☷ with his mission and to care for the poor, until her death in 619 CE. She had borne him six children – two sons called Qasim and Abdallah, who had died in infancy, and four daughters – Zaynab, Ruqayyah, Umm Kulthum and Fatimah.

Khadijah☷ holds a very important position in Islam, as she was one of the first to acknowledge the Prophet Muhammad's mission, and all through the early years, when Muslims were persecuted, she stood by him steadfastly. Her companionship, love and unwavering faith provided him with some of the support that helped him to continue his work through the difficulties. Like her husband, she cared greatly for those in need, and despite their own suffering they always helped and supported those who were tortured and punished for their faith. She was truly a Mother to the Faithful. Khadijah☷ is one of the greatest examples of womanhood and demonstrates the high position that Islam gives to women.

THE ANGEL JIBRIL TELLS MUHAMMAD HIS MISSION

At a certain time each year, Muhammad ☷ left Makkah for a lonely spot a few miles away. He went to the Jabal an-Nur or Mountain of Light, where in the cave of Hira he would spend a period of time alone, fasting and praying. He also liked to give food and money to any poor people who visited him there.

It was during such a time in the month of Ramadan when he was forty years old, that one night the angel Jibril☷ came to him in his sleep. The angel told him to 'Recite' the words that appeared in front of him. Muhammad was bewildered because he was not literate, and was of course unable to read it. The angel Jibril put his arms around him and held him in a strong embrace. Again the angel commanded him to recite those words. He still was not able to read those words. The angel held him even more tightly this time, until Muhammad felt all the breath being squeezed out of him. Yet again the angel commanded Muhammad to recite the words. In desperation, he asked what he should recite. The angel Jibril then recited the following words. These words are now found in the Glorious Qur'an:

RECITE IN THE NAME OF YOUR LORD WHO CREATED. HE CREATED MAN

FROM A CLOT OF BLOOD. RECITE AND YOUR LORD IS THE MOST GENER-
OUS, WHO TAUGHT BY MEANS OF THE PEN, TAUGHT MAN WHAT HE KNEW
NOT.

(Qur'an: 96, 1-5)

Muhammad ﷺ carefully repeated the words after the angel
Jibril until they were deeply carved into his heart and memory.
Only then did the angel depart and the Messenger of Allah ﷺ
awoke.

Muhammad ﷺ was now alone in the darkness. He felt deeply
shaken and confused by what had happened to him. His heart
was beating loudly and he was sure that he was about to die.
What was it that had visited him? Could it have been an evil
spirit? Was he losing his senses? All he wanted to do was to
hurry home to his beloved Khadijah. He had left the cave and
was making his way down the mountain when he was startled to
hear a voice – the same voice that had taught him to recite
those words. His terror returned as he heard the voice proclaim-
ing loudly:

"O Muhammad, you are the Messenger of Allah, and I am
His angel Jibril!"

The words rang out, echoing through the mountains. Muhammad ﷺ looked up to see where the voice was coming from.
Then he saw the angel Jibril. The angel's feet were on the earth
and his head reached high up into the sky. Terrified, the Messenger of Allah looked away. He wanted to escape from this
overpowering vision, but his feet would not move and remained
rooted to the spot. No matter in which direction he looked, all
he could see was the gigantic figure of the angel filling the landscape and sky. The Angel Jibril's words seemed to be reverber-
ating around him and through every atom of his being.

Muhammad ﷺ continued standing there unable to move either forward or backwards – unable to escape. Time itself seemed
to be standing still. His eyes remained fixed on the angel. He
could not tell how long he had been frozen to that spot when the
vision finally disappeared. The Messenger of Allah ﷺ was now
really trembling and felt limp.

Meantime Khadijah had sent a servant to look for her husband, but the servant had returned home not having been able

to find him, so she was pleased to see Muhammad ﷺ when he arrived a little later.

He asked Khadijah to cover him up with a blanket. The vision of the giant figure and the angel's voice resounding through the mountains still filled his senses. He explained to her what had happened. She tenderly comforted him and held him in her arms.

With stops and starts he tried to relate to her what happened, and told her of his fears that he was possessed. She listened attentively to his every word. When she heard what the angel had taught Muhammad to recite, she praised Allah. She soothed him with gentle words and assured him that his vision was not of the devil nor of an evil spirit. She told him that he was a good and pure person, and Allah would never allow an evil spirit to trick him like that.

She believed that it was indeed the angel Jibril who had visited her husband and decided that she must talk to her cousin, Waraqah ibn Nawfal, to ask for his guidance about Muhammad's extraordinary experience. Waraqah ibn Nawfal was a Christian who was probably a unitarian rather than a trinitarian. He was a learned and wise man and had a great understanding of spiritual matters. He also knew from various signs that a prophet was soon to appear among the Arabs. After listening carefully to all that his cousin related, he confirmed that everything that Muhammad ﷺ had experienced was from Allah and that he was indeed the Prophet of Allah. She confirmed her faith in Allah and her belief that her husband is the Messenger of Allah.

Two long years passed by and the Prophet Muhammad ﷺ did not have any further visions. He began to feel lonely and downcast. Could it be that Allah forgotten him? Had it all been a dream? But then at last, he had another revelation. Again he was visited by the angel Jibril who this time brought the following words:

"...YOUR SUSTAINER (ALLAH) HAS NOT FORSAKEN YOU, NOR DOES HE SCORN (YOU); AND, INDEED, THE LIFE TO COME WILL BE BETTER FOR YOU THAN THE EARLIER PART (OF YOUR LIFE)...

DID HE NOT FIND YOU AN ORPHAN, AND GIVE (YOU) SHELTER? AND FOUND YOU LOST ON YOUR WAY, AND GUIDED (YOU)?..."

(Qur'an: 93. 3-4, 6-7)

THE PROPHET MUHAMMAD STARTS HIS MISSION

Through the angel Jibril, Muhammad ﷺ was commanded by Allah to start his task. This he did secretly at first. Khadijah had been one of the first to recognise him as the Prophet. When people later discussed who was the first to accept Islam, they used to say that Khadijah was the first woman, Abu Bakr the first man, Ali the first child and Zaid the first slave to accept Islam ﷺ . She had comforted him after his first vision and had believed him. In fact she had believed in his mission, even before Muhammad ﷺ had been able to accept it. Now she was the first to follow him in prayer – not in a new religion, but in Islam, the way of Allah and of the Prophet Ibrahim ﷺ .

Soon after that the angel Jibril taught the Prophet ﷺ how to do wudu (ablutions) and perform the salah (prayer). The Prophet ﷺ showed Khadijah what the angel Jibril had taught him, and then they prayed together. They did not yet perform the full five prayers that the Muslims perform today because they were revealed much later on the night of the Mi'raj. Another one to join them was ten-year old Ali, the cousin the Prophet ﷺ had adopted. Gradually and in secret, his followers increased, recognising the address of their Lord to them in the rhythm, melody and exquisite language of the Qur'anic verses, and recognising the sublime character of the Messenger of Allah ﷺ . A little later, the Prophet ﷺ began going out among the people of Makkah to call them to turn away from idol-worship and to return to worshipping Allah.

THE NOBLE QUR'AN

Nobody had ever heard any poetry or song which could be compared to these Qur'anic ayat. The Arabs had a great love for poetry and recognised the beauty of the language. As a result some tried to deny the message by saying that the Prophet Muhammad ﷺ was just a very gifted poet. There were people who feared the message the Qur'an brought while others found that they were deeply moved by the ayat. As most were unable to read and write, the ayat were memorised very carefully. The Arabs had a great oral tradition and therefore had excellent memories. Not one word was allowed to be changed. These ayat were then taught to others. Gradually, the few followers – in Islam known as the Companions of the Prophet – who were able to read and write, began to record the ayat – first writing them on the bark and leaves of trees, on bone and on the skins of animals.

The Qur'an was received from Allah in portions. These portions often gave guidance for the problems that the Prophet ﷺ was facing at the time, or about the rules and practice of Islam. The ayat also told of the prophets among the Children of Isra'il who received the previous revelations and who are mentioned in the Jewish books as well as the Old and New Testaments of the Bible. The language of the Qur'an is sometimes metaphorical. Some people tried to assert that the Qur'an was entirely literal in its meanings but the consensus of the Muslims is that some statements within it are metaphorical. Furthermore, as the Prophet ﷺ was Arabic and Allah revealed the Qur'an to him, the words reflect the culture, linguistic usages and land of the Arabs – although the message is never limited to any particular race or peoples.

As in other revelations, Jahannam (the Fire) is described as a terrible, fiery place of great suffering, where wrongdoers go after they die. This wrongdoing however is not merely bad behaviour. Allah is All-Forgiving and may forgive any wrongdoing except for associating something with him as Allah and Lord. Jannah (the Garden) is a luxuriant and beautiful garden with cool rivers running through it. It is a place of milk and honey where the people of tawhid and right action go after death. For an Arab living in the hot and hostile desert, these descriptions of what the Fire and the Garden are like, are particularly clear images that he can understand easily, but they are also just as easily understood by anyone from any culture. For what torture can compare with being burnt in a fire? Then what about eternity in such pain? Everyone knows that one of the most restful and pleasant experiences is to be in the greenery of nature among rivers and plants, particularly in beautiful and well-laid out gardens. So these images were very clear to the Arabs but, of course, they are equally potent to anybody from any culture because the Qur'an is revealed for all humanity until the end of time.

Those who are able to understand the Qur'an in the original Arabic often say that when they read translations of the ayat, they feel as if they are reading a completely different book. Qur'anic Arabic is very different from Western languages and is therefore difficult, if not impossible, to translate accurately. When reading a translation of the Glorious Qur'an, it should be regarded as an interpretation, rather than a translation.

Arabic is an ancient and very pure language and each word can have several subtle differences in meaning. Many scholars also say that the language of the Qur'an has various levels of interpretation. This is why for many centuries people were discouraged from translating the Qur'an into non-Arab languages and Muslims expended great energy in learning Arabic. Even now, people with a greater desire to understand the Book may study for years to try and grasp the meanings of the Book. However, the inner meanings cannot be grasped without a dedication to action to establish Islam in life, purification of behaviour and good character. Muslims generally agree that the way they can benefit most from the Qur'an, apart from embodying it in action and behaviour, is first by listening to it and secondly by chanting it – because to listen to Qur'an when it is recited is an obligation that Allah commands and to recite it is an optional extra act of the Sunnah. The words are the speech of Allah and the very sounds and rhythms help to either calm or stir the feelings and make a person feel awed, happy, fearful, or peaceful and close to Allah, even if he does not understand the Arabic language. By reading the Noble Qur'an it is possible to share in something of the barakah that the Prophet ﷺ received. Some people learn the Qur'an by heart and are regarded with great respect. The name given to such a person is Hafidh.

After the Prophet's death, the written copies of the various surahs (chapters of the Qur'an consisting of ayat or verses) were collected and arranged in order. This was done during the khalifate of Abu Bakr رضي الله عنه and thus within the first two years of the death of the Prophet ﷺ. Then it fell to the Khalifah 'Uthman رضي الله عنه to publish the Qur'an with the surahs in the order we have them now. Later scholars concerned themselves with peripheral matters such as the vowelling of the text, which was necessary for the sake of non-Arabs. This latter process lasted some years and was finalised in about 751 CE. However, the Qur'an was memorised word for word by huge numbers of the Companions in the lifetime of the Prophet ﷺ and it was only that it was recorded textually after his death. The Qur'an contains 114 surahs and 6236 ayat. The surahs were arranged so that, by and large, the longest are at the beginning and the shortest at the end. This is with the exception of the first surah which is quite short. This surah is called the Fatihah, which means 'The Opening'. It is the part of the Qur'an that is recited most often and is included in the five daily prayers. It is regarded as a very special surah.

SURAH 'AL-FATIHAH' (THE OPENING)

IN THE NAME OF ALLAH, MOST BENEFICENT*, MOST MERCIFUL,
PRAISE BE TO ALLAH, THE CREATOR AND SUSTAINER OF THE WORLDS;
THE MOST BENEFICENT, THE MOST MERCIFUL.
MASTER OF THE DAY OF JUDGEMENT,
YOU ALONE DO WE WORSHIP, AND YOU ALONE DO WE BESEECH FOR HELP.
GUIDE US ON THE STRAIGHT PATH,
THE PATH OF THOSE YOU HAVE BLESSED
NOT THE WAY OF THOSE WHO EARN YOUR WRATH,
NOR OF THOSE WHO GO ASTRAY.
* Beneficent means merciful, good, generous, kind.

However, it is difficult to find an accurate translation of the Arabic word, ar-Rahman. Shems Friedlander in his book Ninety-Nine Names of Allah' in his description of this word says that it means "He Who gives blessings and prosperity to all beings..." whereas ar-Rahim denotes the One Who shows compassion to His believing slaves.

The Prophet ﷺ in obedience to the command of Allah in Qur'an, advised people to wash themselves (to take wudu) before reading or reciting the Qur'an. It is necessary to be in a clean and pure state to read the Glorious Book.

When Islam first began to spread, some believed that the Prophet ﷺ was just a gifted poet and had composed the verses himself. However, the Prophet ﷺ was an untutored man who had not been known to compose poetry in the forty years he lived before the revelation. Although he was known for his clarity of speech, since even the greatest of the poets of the age was struck dumb when challenged to create anything to match the amazing nature of the Qur'an, it is unlikely that he could have composed it himself. The Qur'an is the book revealed by Allah to the Prophet Muhammad ﷺ. It is wonderful that there are things that are mentioned in this Noble Book that people did not discover until very recent times, such as the details of how a baby is created and grows in the womb. Allah also speaks of how the moon "borrows" light from the sun, long before people actually discovered that the moon reflects the sun's light (Qur'an 91: 1-2).

NEWS OF ISLAM BEGINS TO SPREAD OUTSIDE MAKKAH

The Quraysh soon began to feel that the Prophet Muhammad's teachings were a threat to them, especially as most of them did not want to give up their gods. They started thinking about how they could prevent this 'new religion' from growing, and how they could stop the Prophet Muhammad ﷺ from talking to people about it. However, Abu Talib, a very well respected and powerful man in the community, gave his nephew his full protection. Because of this, although many in Makkah wanted to punish the Prophet salla'llahu 'alaihi wa sallam, they did not dare harm him. When pilgrims arrived from distant lands, the Quraysh warned them against him. But this had the opposite effect, because when the pilgrims returned home they took news of the Prophet ﷺ and his teachings with them.

BILAL

One of the earliest converts to Islam was an Abyssinian slave called Bilal رضي الله عنه. His master threatened him with terrible things to force him return to the religion of the idols al-Lat and al-Uzza. But Bilal رضي الله عنه took no notice of the threats. As a punishment, he was dragged through the streets with a rough rope around his neck until his flesh was raw and bleeding. He was then beaten. Still Bilal refused to renounce Islam.

The next day his master had him dragged once again through the streets in the scorching midday heat, and threw him down on the burning desert sand. It is said that the sun was so hot that you could cook meat on it. He was stretched out with his hands and feet tied up and was given a lashing. Then just to make sure that he could not survive, a huge rock was placed on his chest, and he was just left there to die. This was not only as a punishment, but it was also as an example to other slaves who might want to follow the Prophet . Still, Bilal ﷜ would not give in. He lay there repeatedly calling out loudly with his powerful, deep voice, "Ahad! Ahad!" – "One! One!". Bilal knew that Allah alone is the One Who decrees good and evil and that there is no-one who can help or harm except Allah.

Abu Bakr ﷜ was a very close companion of the Prophet ﷺ and a devoted Muslim. He passed the spot that day where Bilal was being punished for his faith and was greatly distressed to see how Bilal was made to suffer for being a Muslim. He was also very moved to see the unbending faith of this big, black man. Finding that he could bear it no longer, he decided to offer one of his non-Muslim slaves to Bilal's master in exchange for Bilal. Fortunately, Bilal's master agreed. Abu Bakr was a compassionate and caring man, and took Bilal to his house where he was looked after until he had completely recovered from his injuries. During those days the Prophet ﷺ also visited Bilal to pray for his recovery. Once Bilal had regained his health, Abu Bakr freed him. Abu Bakr also helped other slaves – sometimes he bought them and then freed them. Other times he helped them to buy their freedom.

Bilal became an important figure in the story of Islam. He was always at the side of the Prophet ﷺ . It was his duty to wake the Prophet ﷺ in the morning for the dawn prayer and later he was put in charge of the food supplies for the first armies.

ISRA' AND MI'RAJ

During these troubled times and in the twelfth year of the Prophet's mission, something extraordinary took place. One night when the Prophet Muhammad ﷺ was asleep, he was woken by the angel Jibril. The angel took him to the gates of the courtyard where a shining, winged animal was waiting for him. This animal was called Buraq and looked like a cross between a mule and a donkey. Each stride of the Buraq was so enormous that it reached to the horizon.

The Prophet ﷺ mounted the Buraq and together with the angel Jibril, he travelled to the place in Jerusalem where the Baitu'l-Aqsa and the Mosque of the Dome of the Rock now stand. This mosque stands on the site where the Temple built by the Prophet Sulayman (Solomon)﹏ originally stood. On his arrival there, the Prophet ﷺ lead the other prophets such as Ibrahim (Abraham), Musa (Moses) and 'Isa (Jesus)﹏ in prayer. After this it was time to leave Jerusalem for the next part of his journey with the angel Jibril. The part of the journey that they had just completed is called the 'Night Journey' or 'Isra'.

They then set out on another even more extraordinary journey known as the Mi'raj. Mi'raj means 'Ascension'. This is when the Prophet Muhammad ﷺ journeyed to the highest Heaven.

When we think of somebody going to Heaven, we usually think of this happening after they have died. But when the Prophet ﷺ visited the Seven Heavens, he was alive. He went there and met many of the Prophets, and saw many things of the Unseen, and then was brought into the presence of Allah to such a closeness as no other being in the creation had ever known before him. There he received the five daily prayers from Allah and after it, Allah sent him back to the world to continue the work of renewing and spreading the knowledge, way and practice of the Prophet Ibrahim.

The way that it happened was that after visiting Jerusalem, the Prophet ﷺ mounted the shining Buraq again and guided by the angel Jibril, they flew higher and higher through the night. They flew until they arrived at the First Heaven. As he entered and passed through each of the Seven Heavens, the Prophet Muhammad ﷺ was met and greeted by many of the Prophets that we know from the Qur'an and are also mentioned in the Jewish and Christian books. Among them were Adam, Ibrahim, Yusuf (Joseph), Musa (Moses), and Isa (Jesus)﹏ . The Prophet Muhammad ﷺ as shown the hosts of the angels and the beauty of the Heavens. But he also saw the horrors and burning fires of Hell, where people who had covered over the truth and done wrong during their lives on earth suffered a horrible agony after death.

The Prophet Muhammad ﷺ and the angel Jibril journeyed on until finally, they reached a place beyond which even the angel Jibril could not go. He left the Prophet ﷺ to enter Allah's presence alone. There is a famous difference of views among even the Companions as to whether the Messenger of Allah ﷺ saw Allah, and if he did so whether it was with his eyes or with his heart alone. From comments made by A'ishah, one of the Prophet Muhammad's wives, we receive the impression that the Messenger of Allah ﷺ did not actually see 'the face of Allah'. But other companions were equally sure that he had gazed on the face of his Lord and that this was his distinguishing mark among the Prophets, just as Musa was singled out to hear the speech of Allah directly. Gazing on the face of Allah is something that will be permitted to the best of the right-acting on the Day of Judgement and is the ultimate joy of the next life.

We do not know everything that he experienced there, but one of the things that he was commanded by Allah was to tell the Muslims that they should pray fifty times a day. As the Prophet ﷺ was departing, the Prophet Musa stopped him and asked him what Allah had decreed. When the Prophet Muhammad ﷺ told him, Musa suggested that he should go back to Allah to beg him to lessen the burden for his followers. He told Muhammad ﷺ how difficult it had been to persuade his people to worship Allah when he was on earth. So the Prophet Muhammad ﷺ went back and talked to Allah who agreed to lessen the number to forty.

Once again, as he was leaving, the Prophet Musa stopped him and asked him the same question and when he heard the Prophet's response, the Prophet Musa sent him back to Allah again. This happened several times until the number of prayers was reduced to five times a day.

Yet again, the Prophet Musa pressed him to return to Allah. However, this time, the Prophet Muhammad ﷺ replied that he was too ashamed to go back to Allah another time. Later on, when the Prophet Muhammad ﷺ spoke about this journey, he told his companions that if Muslims prayed five times a day, they would receive a reward equal to praying fifty times a day since every good action is rewarded ten times.

There is some discussion as to how the Prophet ﷺ made this journey. Some people think that the Messenger of Allah ﷺ went with his physical body. Others believe that these journeys were made in the spirit. However, after these experiences, the Prophet ﷺ was able to describe the city of Jerusalem although he had never previously been there. He also described people travelling in a caravan and events that he had seen on the journey. A short time later, the people he had talked about, arrived in Makkah. They were able to confirm that everything that the Prophet ﷺ had described, was true. However, many people still did not want to believe his story and ridiculed him.

THE EXILE OF BANI HASHIM

Life for the Muslims became more and more difficult. The Quraysh even refused to give or sell the Muslims food. The Prophet's refusal to give up his way and his belief in Allah the One turned many people against him. Without Abu Talib the Quraysh became bolder in fighting him and the message he was trying to spread. People jeered at and mocked the Prophet ﷺ and his Companions, and insulted them. They even physically attacked the Prophet ﷺ and the Muslims. One day, the Prophet ﷺ and all his clan (although many were not Muslims) were forced by the Quraysh to move out of the city and live in a barren, stony area. Nobody was allowed even to sell them salt. The Prophet ﷺ was a gentle and kind man, and it hurt him to see how Muslims were insulted and even tortured.

They were only allowed to take with them what they were able to carry on their backs. In the extreme desert conditions, the old and the young suffered the worst. The young would die of heat in the daytime and the old, of cold at night. They built shelters out of thorn bushes, but in the scorching heat of the day, there really was no shade. Despite the fact that people in Makkah were not allowed to help these exiles, some of the Muslims and non-Muslim relatives used secretly to carry food to them.

Without this, they would probably have died.

The Prophet ﷺ realised that it was not possible for the Muslims to continue living under these terrible conditions. With the Prophet's permission, some of the Muslims had escaped to Abyssinia where the Christian king, the Negus, gave them his protection. However, the Prophet ﷺ also decided to approach the town of Ta'if to ask for the protection of its citizens as it was closer than Abyssinia – only about a hundred kilometres away. Instead he was greeted with violence and was chased out of the city under a hail of stones. This period was a severe test of courage and faith for the first Muslims, which they endured with great patience. The tremendous grace they experienced through remembering Allah and the Last Day carried them through their extreme suffering and few people left Islam during those terrible times.

THE YEAR OF SADNESS

619 CE is sometimes called the 'Year of Sadness', because both Khadijah and Abu Talib died. This was a terrible blow for the Prophet ﷺ. In the same year he lost the woman whom he had loved dearly – she had borne him six children, and had been his closest friend and support – and he also lost the uncle who had been his protector through difficult times. Instead of Abu Talib, it was Abu Lahab who became the head of Bani Hashim. He hated Islam and was embarrassed and upset by his nephew's behaviour. He, like many others, thought that the Prophet ﷺ had gone mad. Many different ways were used to try to persuade the Prophet ﷺ to give up his teaching. They offered him wealth and even a high rank in the tribe. However, the Prophet ﷺ replied that if he were given the sun in one hand and the moon in the other, he would still choose Allah.

THE PLEDGE OF 'AQABAH

Some time after that, a delegation of twelve men from a city called Yathrib approached the Prophet ﷺ. There were two main tribes in this city – the Aws and the Khazraj – who were continually at war with each other. The delegation came to ask the Prophet ﷺ to come and live in their city and make peace between the tribes. They met at a place called 'Aqabah. They accepted Islam and pledged allegiance to the Prophet ﷺ with the pledge of allegiance which is known as the First Pledge of 'Aqabah or the Pledge of Women because it involved no promise to fight. However, the Prophet ﷺ could not risk sending all the Muslims to Yathrib, until he was sure of them and the situation in Madinah. So he sent a man called Mus'ab to return with them to teach them about Islam. The Messenger of Allah ﷺ asked the delegation to go back home and if in a year's time they still wished him to go to Yathrib, said that they should return to him.

The year dragged on and seemed like a very long twelve months, while the severe deprivation and suffering of the Muslims did not lessen or ease at all. But the delegation from Yathrib did return exactly one year later. This time there were seventy of them, and they had brought some women with them. At first some of the Muslims thought that this large number was a trap. However, the presence of the women indicated to them that they had nothing to fear. A second secret meeting was held at 'Aqabah. This produced an agreement which was called the Second Pledge of 'Aqabah. The Prophet ﷺ laid down terms on which he would be able to accept their invitation to emigrate. Some of the most important of these terms were:

That they worship Allah without associating anything as a partner with Him;

That the citizens of Yathrib should swear to protect the Prophet ﷺ as they would their own women and children.

The delegation by now knew enough about Islam to know that if the Muslims of Makkah emigrated to their city, the citizens of Yathrib who had taken this pledge, would have to share everything they had with their guests. The only question they asked was, 'What will we get in return?'. The Prophet ﷺ promised them 'Paradise'. Each member of the delegation swore their oath of allegiance to the Prophet ﷺ – both the men and the women, while an almost equal number of Muslims stood as witnesses.

This secret meeting held among rocks in a dry riverbed was a turning point in the history of Islam.

HIJRAH OR EMIGRATION TO MADINAH

The emigration had to be organised very carefully so that it did not attract the attention of the Quraysh. The Muslims were to leave in small groups at different times, travelling by different routes. The Prophet ﷺ himself organised and watched over the arrangements of each departing group. Travelling with children took a little longer – some eleven days on foot. The journey was difficult because everyone was already weak from the three years spent in the desert outside Makkah. However, gradually and a few at a time, they started to arrive in Yathrib to start a new life. With the Prophet's encouragement, nearly all the Muslims emigrated to Madinah, but the Prophet ﷺ stayed on until he received permission from Allah to leave the city of his birth.

In time, Yathrib became known as 'Madinatu'n-Nabi', or the 'City of the Prophet'. This was later shortened to 'al-Madinah', or 'The City'.

THE PROPHET MUHAMMAD PLANS TO LEAVE MAKKAH

Abu Bakr, the Prophet's faithful companion, together with Ali, the Prophet's cousin (who later became his son-in-law) stayed on in Makkah with the Prophet ﷺ. The Quraysh soon realised that most of the Muslims had emigrated to Madinah and decided that they should act without delay and kill the Messenger of Allah ﷺ before he too left Makkah.

A meeting was held of the clans of Quraysh. They agreed that one representative of each tribe would take a sword and all kill him together. By doing it this way, it meant that no one clan of Quraysh could be blamed for the Prophet's death. Although they realised that the Prophet's clansmen might wish to avenge his death, the Quraysh felt sure that as there were so few of them, they would feel outnumbered by the other Quraysh clans. They were confident that the Prophet's clansmen would be quite content to accept blood money as compensation.

However, Allah protected the Prophet ﷺ and guided him not to sleep in his bed that night. The Prophet ﷺ instructed Ali to sleep there instead, wrapped in the Prophet's cloak. As he left the house, the Prophet ﷺ recited an ayah of the Qur'an and threw a handful of dust over his waiting enemies. Miraculously, he passed close to them without being seen. He hurried to Abu Bakr's house who had the camels ready for them to escape from Makkah.

In the early morning, the Quraysh rushed into the Prophet's house to carry out their plan to kill him. But as they reached the bed, they saw that it was brave Ali﹏ who got up from the bed and not the Messenger of Allah. They were extremely angry when they realised that they had been tricked. The Messenger ﹏ had escaped from under their very own eyes!

In the meantime, in the cool desert night, the Prophet ﹏ and Abu Bakr﹏ rode out of Makkah. They travelled as far as they could before it was time to perform their dawn prayers, and then hid in a cave on Mount Thawr. The Quraysh were furious because they had been cheated of their prize, and offered a big reward to anyone who could find the Prophet ﹏ .

In their search, a party of them came right up to the mouth of the cave. They had been guided there by a 'tracker', a man who was expert in tracking people and animals by smell. When they tried to look inside it they saw that the entrance to the cave was blocked. In front of it there was a young acacia tree that had sprung up after the Prophet ﹏ and Abu Bakr had entered it. There was also a big spider's web across the opening, and a pair of doves nesting right in front on the ledge. They decided that there could not be anybody inside the cave, and went away despite the tracker's insistence that they were in the cave. In the Qur'an there are some beautiful ayat that describe what happened and tell of how Allah protected His Messenger ﹏ and Abu Bakr.

The people in Madinah had heard that the Prophet ﹏ and Abu Bakr were on their way and were anxiously watching out for them each day. When the Prophet ﹏ and Abu Bakr with their guide eventually arrived in Madinah, the people greeted them with cries of joy and song. They had been waiting for this moment for a long time. Many were eager to invite the Prophet ﹏ to come and stay with them. Some were very generous and wanted to invite him because they really loved him. But there were also people who realised that if the Prophet ﹏ stayed with them, it would give them a certain status in the community, making them more important in the eyes of others. Whatever the Prophet ﷺ chose to do he would have to avoid taking sides.

The Prophet ﷺ replied to all those who wanted to invite him to be their guest that his camel, Qaswa was under Allah's command, and he must go wherever she took him. He thanked them graciously and blessed them, moving on through the welcoming throng. Finally, the camel stopped on some waste ground used for drying dates, that belonged to two orphaned boys. Before even dismounting, the Prophet ﷺ stopped to thank Allah and asked for His blessings. The Prophet ﷺ exclaimed that this was the spot where he would live and die. This was the spot where he would build his mosque. He called the boys' guardian and paid him an excellent price for the piece of land. In the meantime he stayed for a few days with Abu Ayyub al-Ansari ﷺ the great companion who was later to be buried outside of Constantinople where he had died in the jihad against the Byzantine Romans. His tomb is still there in Istanbul today.

Work started next morning to build the mosque and living quarters for the Prophet ﷺ and his family. Despite his long and dangerous journey, the Prophet ﷺ actively helped with the building. The work proceeded so quickly with song and such vibrant energy, that onlookers said that they looked as if they were dancing rather than building. A mosque still exists on this spot today although it has been rebuilt and greatly enlarged. One account tells of how the Prophet ﷺ lifted a child up and helped him to put one brick into position, laughing and saying that now the child could say that he had helped the Prophet ﷺ to build the mosque!

Chapter 3: Madinah & the Struggle to Establish Islam

MADINAH 'THE RADIANT' – THE FIRST MUSLIM COMMUNITY

The first mosque was built in Quba', near Madinah. The second was the Prophet's Mosque. This was a simple building made with a foundation of stones, walls of sun-dried bricks, and a roof of palm leaves supported by the trunks of palm trees, which the Prophet ﷺ himself helped to build. This mosque quickly became the centre of the Muslim community in Madinah. In fact, this was the first Muslim community ever to exist. It was the first time that Muslims were able to pray openly, practise their way freely and live without fear of punishment.

When the Muslims of Makkah emigrated to Madinah, they left their homes without taking any of their belongings with them so as not to attract the attention of their persecutors. Many of them had been close to the condition of those who live in the desert and had virtually no belongings by today's standards. They were called Muhajirun – emigrants – in Arabic. The Messenger of Allah forged bonds of brotherhood between individuals of the Muhajirun and of the people of Madinah, and the Muslims of Madinah adopted the emigrants as blood brothers and sisters. Everything they owned was shared equally. These Muslims of Madinah became known as 'Ansar', which means 'Helpers' or 'those who give succour'.

The true feeling of brotherhood in Islam started to grow in Madinah. This is the basis of the community or 'Ummah', and it was probably the first time for hundreds of years in Arab history that people began to feel united through their worship of Allah, the One. Their loyalty was no longer first to their own tribe, but to Allah, and to the Messenger of Allah ﷺ and their Muslim brothers and sisters. The arrival of Islam did not abolish the values of tribal loyalty but it placed it within the wider perspective of obedience to Allah and His Messenger ﷺ.

BILAL BECOMES THE FIRST MU'ADHDHIN

It was during the years in Madinah, that many of the judgements of the shari'ah were revealed. To build this first Muslim community, the Prophet ﷺ had to work hard to wipe out old pagan customs and enmities.

Prayers could now be done openly at the mosque and at the appointed times. In those days, however, people did not have watches, so it was difficult for them to know exactly when they had to be at the mosque. It often happened that some people would have already started the prayers when others would be arriving. The problem was how to call people to prayer so that they all arrived together.

One day, one of the Muslims had a dream which he related to the Messenger of Allah ﷺ. The Prophet ﷺ understood that this dream was guidance from Allah telling the Muslims that they should not use a bell or other instrument for calling people to prayer. Instead, Muslims should be called to prayer using the human voice. The Prophet ﷺ told Bilal, the former Abyssinian slave with a powerful and beautiful voice, to become the first 'mu'adhdhin' – the man who has the duty to call Muslims to prayer at the correct time.

These days, in a few of the Muslim countries, a mu'adhdhin is sometimes also called a 'bilal', in memory of the former slave. The call to prayer is called the 'adhan'. From that moment, five times a day, Bilal's strong, melodious voice would call the Muslims of Madinah to prayer. They heard Bilal's voice in every corner of the city, and hurried to the mosque to pray together. As Islam spread to other places and other countries, a mu'adhdhin would be chosen by the local Muslims. Since that time, all over the world, Muslims have been called to prayer by the adhan, five times a day, every day.

WHAT PEOPLE HAVE TOLD US ABOUT THE PROPHET

People have described the Prophet ﷺ as being of between

tall and medium height, of a slim build with broad shoulders. His skin was light and his hair black and slightly curly reaching to his ear lobes. He also had a beard. Even in old age he hardly had any grey hair. His eyes were very dark with long lashes and arched eyebrows. Between his shoulder-blades there was a birth-mark which was the 'Seal of Prophethood'. When he walked he strode and the earth seemed to roll away from under his feet. When standing or walking his body leaned forward slightly. He often smiled, although underlying that was an expression of grav-ity. When he turned to talk to somebody, he turned his whole body to face the person and his manner was always courteous, humble and gentle. His most notable feature, was the radiance that shone from his face and eyes

When people first met him they would be filled with awe. But in a short time they found themselves completely charmed by him and very soon after that they would become devoted to him. The Ummah has a deep and unwavering love for their Pro-phet. Even most of his enemies, in the end, pledged their alle-giance to him. He did not like people to flatter him, and forbade them to prostrate themselves before him – or after his death, at his tomb. When somebody called him 'Lord', he replied quickly that only Allah was 'Lord'. It is Muslim practice to regularly pray for the Prophet Muhammad ﷺ , as well as all the other prophets out of gratitude for everything we have received from him and through him.

He was known for his great love, compassion and patience, and for always speaking the truth – even Abu Sufyan who was one of the Prophet's worst enemies until he became a Muslim, said that the Prophet ﷺ had never told a lie. The Prophet ﷺ was always ready to be supple and yielding in order to make peace as long as it did not go against Islam and the Will of Allah. He always carried out the terms of any treaty he had agreed, and always trusted the Almighty. In all dealings he was just and fair. He was never the aggressor in any war.

He had a very tender heart. When someone once related to him how a father had buried his young daughter while she was crying out to him, the Prophet ﷺ dissolved into tears. He never took revenge on anybody who had hurt him, and even allowed the woman who had tried to poison him, to go without punishment. Truly, he was an example of compassion.

The Prophet ﷺ had great humility and helped with the housework, mended his own clothes and shoes, milked the goat, cooked occasionally and looked after the children. He was a loving father and husband and encouraged the male members of his Ummah to also treat their wives and children with tenderness and understanding. He told them that the greatest charity they could do was to look after and care for them.

The Prophet ﷺ loved children and did not approve of parents beating them unnecessarily, although it is well known that he ordered parents to beat older children who failed to do their prayers. After his death, his widow, A'ishah﷽ , would sometimes relate how when she was still little she would play with her dolls and the Prophet ﷺ would sometimes join in. Other times if she was playing with her friends, he would encourage them to go on. Taking great delight, he watched them from a distance. On occasion, the Prophet ﷺ and A'ishah﷽ even raced each other.

Both Muslim and non-Muslim children were very welcome in his home, since every child is close to the natural condition known in Arabic as the fitrah. He said, "Islam is the way of the fitrah." Often when his daughter, Fatimah﷽ , came into the room, he would stand up, kiss her on the forehead, and give her his seat. She would do likewise for her father. When he returned from a journey or some battle, he would often pick up a couple of children, set them down in front of him on his camel and give them a ride. Once it happened that when the Prophet ﷺ was praying in the mosque, a child started clambering all over him. However, he never chided the child.

He always fought for the weak in society, and preferred to give his food to someone who asked for it than enjoy the meal himself. In fact, often as a result of this, there was no food in his home, and he and his family went to bed hungry. Once he had started on his mission, he probably never went to bed with a full stomach. People have related that sometimes he would tie a stone (or two) to his stomach to get some relief from hunger pangs.

However, the Messenger ☙ also often advised people that they should look after their bodies. Sometimes, in their fervour to reach Paradise, Muslims would fast all the time. The Prophet ☙ forbade this, perhaps as being dangerous for their health. The times in Madinah were sometimes very hard and if the Prophet ☙ d not eat, it was because he could not bear to see his neighbour go hungry while he was satisfied. In the same way, the Prophet ☙ frowned on extravagance, and made sure that neither he nor his family were ever wasteful. A'ishah☙ said that if they had oil in their house it would only be used for cooking. To economise, they would not even light a lamp.

The Prophet ☙ cared very much for each person in his Ummah, and was always there for anybody who needed his help. He treated people completely fairly. He helped slaves buy their freedom, and gave money to a Muslim who could not afford a dowry so that he could get married. He even asked A'ishah to give whatever food they had in the house for the wedding feast. That night A'ishah☙ and the Prophet ☙ had no food at all.

The Messenger of Allah☙ helped people to understand that Allah does not look on the outward forms of people but on their hearts and inward. This understanding helped the great and strong Muslims not to become arrogant and to know that it is their duty to protect the weak. Although in those days and all throughout Islamic history people kept slaves, he taught the Muslims that their slaves are not to be beaten. They are also not allowed to be overburdened with work. If the work is too much, then the master of the house should help. They are to eat with the family and are to be given the same kind of food that the family eat. They are to be clothed as the family are clothed. To encourage people to free their slaves, the Messenger of Allah ☙ told them of the rewards they would receive in Heaven if they do so. He himself set a clear example when he appointed Bilal, a black man and former slave, to high office. Indeed throughout Islamic history many of the most distinguished men and women have been former slaves or the sons and daughters of slaves.

He sought advice and counsel regarding all sorts of things – even matters of governance and strategies for battles, and would always listen carefully to each person's view. However, once he had taken a decision, the Ummah would support it fully.

He insisted that people should be kind to their animals, and said that no animal should ever be killed without good reason. They should never be tortured. Once when his army was on the march, he diverted the soldiers away from where a bitch lay suckling her young pups.

He taught the Muslims to be a responsible community, to look after each other and to love each other. He used to tell people with regard to their faith: "None of you (truly) believes until he loves for his brother what he loves for himself."

THE PROPHET AND HIS WIVES – THE 'MOTHERS OF THE FAITHFUL'

After Khadijah's death روهي , the Prophet صلى took several wives. Except for A'ishah روهي , Abu Bakr's daughter, all his other wives were widows and one was a divorcee. It sometimes happened that he married them at their request to give them his protection when they lost their husbands. These marriages also helped to make peace between the tribes. The wife's tribe became related to the Prophet's tribe or family. This meant that there had to be peace between them. One of his wives came from a Christian community and another from a Jewish. They both became Muslims when they married the Messenger of Allah صلى .

The wives all shared the simplicity in which the Prophet صلى chose to live, and they themselves, became well known for their generosity and purity. They frequently fasted and devoted their time to prayer and looking after the needy. When one of them once complained because their lives were so simple, the Prophet صلى said that if they were not happy with him, he could divorce them. But none chose that. They all chose to share his difficult life, which often meant sharing with others everything that they had. This is what the Prophet صلى did all the time.

To the end, Prophet Muhammad صلى always remembered Khadijah روهي . He could never forget that she was the person who had stood by him and supported him in the very early days. His love remained so deep that when he heard a voice that was similar to Khadijah's or was reminded of her by a necklace, tears would well up in his eyes.

The Prophet's wives were known as The Mothers of the Faithful because Allah named them as such in the Qur'an.

PEOPLE OF THE BENCH

There were a number of poor people in the Muslim community who had nowhere to live and no money to buy food. They were young men who chose to live as close to the Messenger of Allah ﷺ as possible in order to benefit from his company and to learn as much of their deen as they could. Many of them are now famous for their great wisdom and learning. As more people accepted Islam and emigrated to Madinah, their numbers increased. One of the colonnades of the mosque was given to them and this became their home. The Prophet ﷺ and his family whose quarters were attached to the Mosque, felt that they were responsible for these people. They and any others who lived close by were never able to eat a proper meal as they were always concerned that these people should not go hungry. The Prophet used to say that a meal for one is enough for two, a meal for two is enough for four, and a meal for four is enough for eight.

These people who lived in the Mosque were given a stone bench for their use. As a result, they became known as the People of the Bench.

Each day in the mosque, they would keep company with the Prophet ﷺ and pay particular attention if he were to recite, teach or explain something about the Noble Qur'an – in time they became very knowledgeable. Later, the Prophet ﷺ sometimes sent them to distant lands to govern people who had become Muslims or to teach them or to call people to Islam. After his death, people came to them to learn about their Islam and for advice. Many had become knowledgeable in reciting and explaining the meaning of the Noble Book. Through keeping the company of the Prophet ﷺ and absorbing his teaching they had also become teachers of the beliefs and practices of Islam.

THE FIGHT FOR THE SURVIVAL OF ISLAM

Although at last, the Muslims were able to worship Allah freely, they still had many problems. Many of the Muhajirun who had once been rich now had nothing. Any property or goods that they had left behind had been seized by the Quraysh. They depended entirely on the support of the Ansar. Also, many could no longer do the work they used to do when they lived in Makkah. The people of Makkah were largely traders while the inhabitants of Madinah mainly grew date palms and other crops. It became harder and harder to survive for both the Muhajirun and the Ansar.

The greatest threat to the Muslims continued to be the Quraysh who did not like the fact that Islam was growing and were determined to destroy it. They were powerful and could easily wipe out the small number of Muslims in Madinah. They also continued to oppress and torture any Muslims who had been left behind in Makkah. The Ka'bah had always been a place of refuge and nobody had the right to prevent anyone from visiting it. However, the Quraysh were preventing Muslims from worshipping there. The Prophet ﷺ tried to make treaties with neighbouring tribes and communities, as was the custom among the Arabs. He wanted peace, not war. But sometimes these tribes and communities joined the enemy instead. Some pretended to be allies of the Muslims, but secretly supported the enemy. These people and others who pretended to be Muslims but were really disbelievers were called hypocrites. Life was very dangerous. It was against this background that the Prophet had a revelation which allowed the Muslims to fight.

"PERMISSION IS GRANTED TO THOSE WHO FIGHT BECAUSE THEY HAVE BEEN OPPRESSED, AND ALLAH WILL AID THOSE WHO HAVE BEEN DRIVEN FROM THEIR HOMES MERELY FOR SAYING 'OUR LORD IS ALLAH'."
(Qur'an: 22.39)

Before this, during the years of persecution and hardship when the Muslims had borne their suffering with submission and patience, the Prophet ﷺ had received a revelation, which had advised him to deal gently with the disbelievers, and to give them respite for a while. But now the survival of Islam and their own survival depended on their willingness to fight. It was no longer right that they should submit to the evil that the Quraysh were inflicting on them. It was clear that they had to fight back in order to conquer that evil. Permission to fight had to be understood as a command. Another revelation that came soon after was indeed a command from Allah that the Muslims should fight their enemies until there was no further persecution, and the way of Allah prevailed over all other ways. This meant that they should fight the idolaters and not the People of the Book, the Jews and the Christians who at that time had treaties with the Muslims. Later, the command came to fight the People of the Book if they did not accept Islam or agree to live under Muslim governance. During the battles that later took place for the survival of Islam, the loyalty and faith of these early Muslims were put to the test. Even the Prophet ﷺ lost many people from among his own family and friends.

RAIDS ON THE QURAYSH CARAVANS

The Prophet was faced with a difficult problem. If the small band of Muslims took on the Quraysh in a proper battle, they would have little chance of surviving, and certainly even less chance of defeating them. The only alternative was to try and weaken the Quraysh economically. The Quraysh made their money by trading and regularly sent caravans across the desert to places like Syria. They had also made a lot of money from the property that they had seized from the Muhajirun, so the Messenger of Allah ﷺ decided that the best way of weakening the Quraysh was to attack their caravans and to take their merchandise.

THE BATTLE OF BADR – THE FIRST BATTLE AGAINST QURAYSH

One day, news reached Madinah of a very large caravan returning to Makkah from Syria, in the charge of a powerful leader of the Quraysh called Abu Sufyan. The Prophet ﷺ decided that they would attack this caravan. He rode out to the Well of Badr near the Red Sea, with three hundred and thirteen Muhajirun and Ansar. The goods Abu Sufyan was bringing back to Makkah, were worth a lot of money, and he wanted to return to Makkah safely. So as he travelled he made enquiries to find out whether there was any danger in the area, and he soon heard of the Muslims' plan.

Abu Sufyan immediately decided to take a different route and sent a man called Dhamdham, from a local tribe, to hurry to Makkah to warn the Quraysh. Most of the people of Makkah had invested their money in this caravan and they were extremely worried when Dhamdham arrived with this terrible news. They were so outraged that without any hesitation, they put on their armour. By that evening, a thousand men led by most of the important and powerful people in Makkah, were on their way to Badr.

News of the Quraysh army quickly reached the Prophet Muhammad. He decided to call a meeting of all those who were with him. These enthusiastic Muslims had not come out with him to fight a proper battle and were not equipped for it. The Prophet Muhammad ﷺ needed to be sure that everyone wanted to stay to fight. The Quraysh would be wearing their best armour, while the Prophet's men wore armour made of tree bark. The Quraysh army would consist of people who were relatives of the Emigrants. Would the Emigrants be willing to fight them? The Ansar also did not have any quarrel with the Quraysh; would they want to be involved in the battle?

However, both the Muhajirun and the Ansar promised to stand by the Prophet ﷺ and fight. They told the Prophet ﷺ that if he told them to jump into the sea, they would do this! They loved and trusted the Messenger of Allah ﷺ completely. The small 'army' of Muslims made their way to the Well of Badr. When they arrived there they found two water-carriers who told them about the number of men in the Makkan army. They were so horrified that at first the Muslims did not believe the men.

Meantime, Abu Sufyan took the caravan to safety and then let the Makkan army know that they should go home. However, Abu Jahl, one of the army leaders was an arrogant, ambitious man and refused to turn back. He could only think of the glory he would gain by destroying the Prophet Muhammad ﷺ. He wanted to go to Badr and hold three days of feasting and drinking there. He promised there would be girls to make music and entertain the fighting men. He felt sure that all the Arabs would respect him for this in the future. However, some of the tribes in the Makkan army did not want to fight now that the caravan was safe and decided to return home. The rest, about a thousand men, followed Abu Jahl.

When the Makkan army had set up camp in Badr, Abu Jahl sent 'Umayr to spy on the Muslim army. When 'Umayr saw them he was filled with terror. Though the Muslim army was so much smaller, Umayr saw the determined expression on the men's faces. He also saw 'camels carrying Death'. He tried to persuade Abu Jahl to change his mind. Others, who may also have had some premonition, in their turn tried to dissuade Abu Jahl from going to battle. The Arabs traditionally preferred to find a way to make peace, rather than fight and lose a lot of men in a battle. They also did not want to kill members of their own families. Still Abu Jahl would not listen. He was a proud man and scorned them, calling them 'cowards'.

From his position by the well, Prophet Muhammad ﷺ could not see the size of the Makkan army. He had chosen this position to prevent the Makkans from reaching the water. It also meant that when the battle started the Makkans would have the sun in their eyes. This would give the Prophet's army the advantage. Then suddenly it rained. This made the ground firm for the Prophet's army, but very slippery for Abu Jahl's men who had to climb up the hill.

In the morning light, when the Prophet ﷺ saw the full size of the Makkan army, he prayed to Allah for help. If this tiny army were destroyed, it would mean that there would be no people on the earth left to worship Allah! The Prophet ﷺ had not lifted his sword against anyone before. He put all his faith in Allah and gave strict instructions as to how his army was to fight.

As the two armies came face to face, Abu Jahl taunted the Muslims, hurling all sorts of insults at them. In those days, battles were usually started by about two or three men from one side challenging the same number of men from the other side. Only after that did the leaders give the command that the armies should start fighting each other. However, Abu Jahl refused to let his three Quraysh generals fight the three Ansar that came forward. He only wanted to fight the Muhajirun. So three Muhajirun came out and killed the three Quraysh generals within seconds. One Muslim was mortally wounded.

The Prophet ﷺ then gave the command for his army to attack and the two armies started battling with each other. The
Muslims fought with great discipline and determination – the
Prophet ﷺ had drilled them well. The Makkans had no discipline, and were led by different leaders. When they tried to reach
the well, they were met by showers of arrows shot by the Prophet's men. At one point the Prophet ﷺ took a handful of sand
and flung it at the Quraysh. He told his men that Jibril together
with a thousand angels were attacking the army. Suddenly a
wind raised the burning sand into the eyes and faces of the Quraysh. Above the noise of the battle could be heard the voices of
the Muslims shouting 'Allahu Akbar!', 'Allah is the Most Great!'.
Soon Abu Jahl was dead and the Quraysh fled in panic, leaving
some fifty dead.

This battle can be regarded as a miracle, because the Muslim
army was so small, yet with Allah's help they were able to defeat a much larger and stronger one. It was also a terrible em-
barrassment for the Quraysh that they were beaten by so few
men.

JIHAD

The Battle of Badr was fought during Ramadan in 624 CE. It
was the first battle in the Jihad. Jihad is an Arabic word meaning 'a struggle', although in the West people think it just means
'a Holy War'. In the Muslim sense it means 'a struggle against
wrong', or 'striving in the cause of Allah'. It does not only mean
to fight wrong as in a battle although this is the highest form of
jihad. In fact, one day when a woman called Umm Anas asked
the Prophet ﷺ for advice for her life, the Prophet ﷺ replied:
"Forsake all wrongs for they are the best to forsake. Adhere to
religious duties, for they are the best form of jihad". Jihad, therefore, also means to struggle against the bad within ourselves,
although it must also be remembered that the Messenger of Allah
ﷺ was speaking to a woman and of course she was not obliged
to struggle in warfare as are the men. So if Muslims adhere to
their acts of worship and stick within the shari'ah, it helps them
to control the negative side of their natures. Physical jihad, however, is not only permitted in certain circumstances as when a

country is under attack, or Muslims are in physical danger or if they are prevented from practising or spreading their religion in a peaceful manner. Among the last revelations were those which made jihad obligatory on the Muslims against the disbelievers – the People of the Book – until the end of time. That jihad has the obligatory precondition that they must invite them to become Muslims, and if they refuse that they must be offered the opportunity of living under the governance of the Muslims while paying the jizyah. If, however, they refuse that, they must be fought

PRISONERS

During the raids and battles prisoners were often taken. The Qur'anic revelation after Badr allowed the Messenger of Allah ﷺ a number of options in his treatment of the prisoners: either to execute them, enslave them, free them totally or ransom them. The Prophet Muhammad ﷺ treated the prisoners of Badr in the following manner:

If ransoms could be paid for the prisoners by their families, this was best. However, if a prisoner taught fifteen children to read and write he was set free. The Prophet ﷺ placed a truly high value on education. If the prisoners were kept captive until the ransom was paid they had to be looked after like members of the family, although they would still have to be bound. A prisoner could not be made to walk if his captor was riding a camel or horse. Prisoners were killed only if there was a very good reason. After some of the battles, they were killed for committing acts of treachery or because they endangered the lives of the Muslims. Some prisoners became Muslims because they were so impressed by the way they were treated.

The rules concerning women and children who might be encountered during the fighting, were especially strict. The Prophet ﷺ gave orders that neither women nor children were ever to be harmed unless they actively took a part in the fighting.

THE BATTLE OF UHUD

The Battle of Uhud took place about a year after the Battle of Badr. The Quraysh put all the profits from the caravan that was the cause of the Battle of Badr, into creating a strong army.

Three thousand men under the command of Abu Sufyan marched to Madinah to get their revenge after the Battle of Badr. They were determined to completely destroy the Muslims and their way.

This battle turned out to be a great disaster for the Muslims. Some of the seven hundred Muslims felt very confident after the Battle of Badr, and did not wish to listen when the Prophet Muhammad ﷺ suggested that they barricade themselves in the city. The young champions were full of pride after the great victory of Badr, and they could not wait to face the enemy and fight. Initially, the battle was an overwhelming success for the Muslims who were again greatly outnumbered. However, this time there was a lack of discipline among them. Some forgot that they were fighting for Allah and for the survival of Islam. They became greedy and were only interested in getting their share of the booty.

As a result, the Quraysh won the battle and many Muslims were lost including some of their best fighters. The Quraysh thought that they had killed the Prophet ﷺ and were preparing to return to Makkah. However, the Prophet ﷺ had only been wounded and was still alive. When Abu Sufyan heard this news, he promised to meet the Muslims at Badr the following year.

The Prophet ﷺ was concerned that they might return and attack Madinah again, so he asked the Muslims who had fought in this battle to accompany him to give chase. Although many were very badly wounded, they prepared themselves and followed the Quraysh army. At night they built and lit hundreds of fires which gave the impression to Abu Sufyan and his army that there were many more of them. The Quraysh decided to hurry home.

The year after the Battle of Uhud, 626 CE was a difficult and testing time for the Prophet ﷺ and his Ummah. They had lost many people in the Battle of Uhud and seemed to be surrounded by enemies. People plotted to take the Prophet's life. His followers were ambushed. Friends and allies of the Muslims, sometimes secretly became friends of the enemy. These people, and the group of people who had outwardly become Muslims but were really still disbelievers, were called munafiqun – hypocrites.

The defeat at the Battle of Uhud, the loss of so many Muslims and the difficulties that the Ummah faced in Madinah, were hard to bear. Morale was very low. It was during this period that some ayat of the Qur'an were revealed to the Prophet ﷺ in which Allah, glorious and exalted is He, spoke of what had happened at Uhud when some of the Muslims became greedy for booty and forgot they were fighting for the sake of Allah and for the survival of Islam. This had endangered everyone's lives and resulted in the defeat. These ayat include:

"So lose not heart,
Nor fall into despair:
For you must gain mastery
If you are true in faith."

(Qur'an 3: 139)

"Did you think that you
Would enter the Garden
Without Allah testing
Those of you who fought hard
(In His cause) and
Remained steadfast."

(Qur'an 3: 142)

These ayat gave comfort – the Muslims knew that in the end they would be victorious. But the ayat also explained that it is not always easy on Allah's Path, and sometimes there must be tests. Tests are necessary to grow strong and to prove one's devotion to Allah.

SHAHEEDS

The early Muslims were filled with a strong faith in Allah, the Almighty. They loved Allah with their whole beings and strove to live according to His Will, no matter what the cost. They knew that their leader, the Prophet Muhammad ﷺ was truly the Messenger of Allah and trusted him completely.

The Prophet ﷺ really desired peace. But Arabia was a disunited and lawless country, without any well-ordered government. Many of the Arab tribes were determined to destroy Islam, so that to survive, the Muslims had to fight. Although, many Muslims died in these wars, they never held back or hesitated, because they knew that the next life could only be better than this. They had given up their old way of living and now lived according to the Qur'an and the Prophet's sunnah. They had been commanded to fight until persecution was ended and everyone worshipped Allah the One. The Qur'an stated that nobody could die unless it was Allah's Will. Also, if anybody died fighting a jihad, he would become a shaheed – a witness – and be given a place in Paradise.

THE BATTLE OF THE TRENCH

The following year, the Prophet ﷺ and his army travelled to Badr as they had promised. They encamped there for a number of days to meet Abu Sufyan. Because there was a severe drought, Abu Sufyan could not keep his promise and his threat to meet the Muslims in Badr. The drought meant that there would not be enough food for the animals and travelling would be very difficult. He was too embarrassed to tell the Prophet ﷺ that he and his army could not come, but by not letting the Prophet ﷺ know, he was in a worse position. In fact, he had become the laughing stock of the country. He became even more determined to carry out his threat.

As soon as he was able to, he gathered together an enormous army of ten thousand men and set out to attack Madinah. Although the Prophet ﷺ had only three thousand men, he decided that this time they would defend Madinah and called a meeting to discuss how they would do this. They realised that the south and southeast of the city could easily be attacked, but could not decide how best to defend these areas.

Among the Muslims was a former slave called Salman. The young Persian had been helped by the Prophet ﷺ and his Companions to buy his freedom. He had been listening to the discussions intently and decided to put forward his idea of how they could solve their problem. He explained how in Persia they dug big, wide trenches around their cities to withstand sieges. Everyone was delighted with his idea and started digging. Even the Prophet ﷺ dug with them while he led them in song.

When the Quraysh arrived they were very taken aback and did not know what to make of the trench. They had never seen

anything like this before. The leaders of the Makkan army discussed and argued about how they should attack. Finally, they
decided that the cavalry should try to jump the trench. The great
horses leaped across, but as soon as they landed on the other
side the horsemen were cut down by the Muslims. This went on
day after day and the Makkan army and animals began to suffer
from the heat and lack of food. There was also disagreement
among the Quraysh and their allies. Then suddenly one day the
weather changed and chill winds began to blow. This was followed by cold winter rain. Abu Sufyan, his army and the animals began to fall ill. They decided to go home.

TREATY OF HUDAYBIYYAH 628 CE

One day after the month of Ramadan, during the month of
Shawwal, the Prophet ﷺ dreamt that he entered the Ka'bah
with shaven head. He also had the key of the Ka'bah in his hand.
On waking he called his companions together and announced
that he was going to Makkah to make the Lesser Pilgrimage or
'Umrah, and invited his companions to join him. The Hajj is the
Greater Pilgrimage which can only be performed at a certain
time each year. The 'Umrah can be performed at any time of
the year.

There was great excitement as preparations were made for
the journey. Seventy camels were bought to be sacrificed in
Makkah – the meat would be distributed among the poor of the
city. In a very short time they were ready to depart. The Prophet was alr eady in ihram, the dress of the pilgrim which con-
sists of two lengths of white cloth, and his head was bare. Some
of his companions wanted to go armed, because they were afraid
that the Quraysh might attack them. But the Prophet ﷺ insisted that they only carry their usual hunting swords.

As they set out, they heard from a scout sent ahead by the
Prophet ﷺ that the Quraysh had sent a troop of two hundred
horses to obstruct their progress. With the help of a man from
another tribe, they made their way towards Makkah by a different route. They had just reached the edge of Hudaybiyyah when
the Prophet's camel, Qaswa, lay down and refused to move.
People thought that she was just being obstinate, but the Pro-

phet ☙ knew that she was under Allah's guidance. He understood that they should go no further and commanded everyone to encamp in Hudaybiyyah which was a flat area lying close to Makkah.

The Quraysh thought that the Prophet ☙ and his followers had come to do battle. They could not believe that they had only come to perform the 'Umrah. This gave rise to many exchanges between representatives of the Quraysh and the Prophet ☙. The Quraysh were adamant that they would not allow the Muslims into Makkah. They had just had a severe defeat at the Battle of the Trench and were still smarting from this experience.

They were in a dilemma. If they did not allow the Muslims to perform their pilgrimage, this would be against the ancient laws of the Ka'bah and the surrounding sacred ground. They, as keepers of the Ka'bah, had the duty to ensure that anybody wishing to make the pilgrimage was allowed to do so without coming to any harm.

On the other hand, if they allowed the Muslims into Makkah, this would give the Prophet ☙ and his people an enormous moral victory. Whatever, the Quraysh decided, their reputation would be badly affected and all Arabia would soon know about it. So when two of their own representatives visited the Muslim camp and returned with the advice that the Quraysh should indeed allow the pilgrimage to go ahead, the leaders still felt that they could not permit it.

Finally, the Quraysh sent a man called Suhayl to conclude a treaty between the Muslims and themselves. At first, problems arose because the Prophet ☙ wanted to begin the document with the words "In the Name of Allah, the Beneficent, the Merciful". Despite the protests of his companions, the Messenger of Allah ☙ agreed to the wording: "In Thy Name, O Allah". Suhayl also did not want the Prophet's name to be written as "Muhammad, Messenger of Allah". So the Prophet ☙ agreed to "Muhammad, son of Abdallah". During these negotiations, the Prophet ☙ showed immense patience and willingness to yield and be supple for the sake of peace. Many of his companions were outraged by the demands of the Quraysh and could not understand why the Prophet ﷺ agreed to them. At last the terms of the treaty were agreed. In outline, they were:

There would be no war between the two parties (the Muslims and the Quraysh) for a period of ten years;

The Muslims would not be allowed to perform the 'Umrah that year, but they could return the following year. The Quraysh would leave the city and allow the Muslims three days in Makkah, to complete their 'Umrah. When going to perform 'Umrah, the Muslims would only be allowed to carry sheathed swords. No other weapons would be permitted;

If a Muslim escaped from the Quraysh, the Prophet ﷺ had to return the person to the Quraysh. However, if a Muslim wished to return to the Quraysh, they should be allowed to do this, but the Quraysh would not have to send the person back to the Muslims;

Any tribes wishing to make alliances with either the Quraysh or the Muslims would be free to do so.

Some of the Muslims felt that this treaty was very unfair because most of the terms were in favour of the Quraysh. However, the Prophet ﷺ did not see this as a personal war and simply followed the guidance he received from Allah the Almighty. He knew that Allah would guide them to what was best for them. This was an example of how far the Prophet ﷺ would go in order to make peace – as long as it was in accordance with the Will of Allah.

The Muslims' spirits rose when a young man, a Muslim called Abu Jandal who had escaped from Makkah, arrived at the camp. But he was Suhayl's son. Unfortunately, Abu Jandal arrived just after the treaty had been signed, so the Prophet ﷺ had to agree that he return to Makkah with his father. Although the two other Quraysh representatives promised to look after him and protect him from his father's wrath, the Muslims found this incident very upsetting and frustrating.

Once the treaty was signed, the Prophet ﷺ commanded that everybody should sacrifice their animals, shave or trim their hair and change out of ihram. Nobody moved. They just stared at him. Things had not turned out the way they had expected. And now the Prophet ﷺ was asking them to do something which was not in accordance with the rules and rituals of the pilgrimage. They must have felt very confused.

The Prophet ﷺ was very upset by their reaction and went into his tent. This was the first time the Muslims had not immediately followed his command. Umm Salamah ﵂ , one of his wives who had accompanied him on this journey, suggested that he himself should go out to sacrifice his animal, shave his head and change out of ihram. She felt sure that everybody would follow his example. He followed her advice and immediately, everybody seemed to spring to life and rushed to do as he did. Soon the whole camp was strewn with locks of hair. Suddenly there was a strong gust of wind that lifted up all the hair and carried it to Makkah. The Muslims now understood why the Prophet ﷺ had commanded them to carry out the rituals. This was a sign that their pilgrimage had been accepted by Allah

The Prophet ﷺ sometimes said that when the time came for people's actions to be judged by Allah, He would judge them by the intention rather than the actions alone. The Muslims had journeyed to Makkah with the intention of making their pilgrimage. However, due to the various difficulties that had arisen, they were prevented from carrying it out. Allah, in His Mercy, had accepted their intention, – it was not their fault that they had been prevented from performing this ritual.

AFTER THE TREATY OF HUDAYBIYYAH

The Muslims returned to Madinah with mixed feelings. Many were not happy with the terms of the treaty. They did not like the Quraysh to have such an advantage. However, there were soon developments that made the Quraysh wish that they had not demanded one particular condition of this treaty.

During the two years in which this treaty held, it became much easier for the Prophet ﷺ to carry on his work. Most of the restrictions had been removed. This allowed the number of Muslims to double. There were expeditions to other towns and cities and the influence of Islam began to spread far and wide. The Prophet ﷺ also exchanged letters with the Negus of Abyssinia and rulers of other countries bordering Arabia. In these letters the Prophet ﷺ called on the rulers to accept Islam.

At this time in Makkah there lived a man called Abu Baseer. He became a Muslim after being deeply moved when he heard the Qur'an being recited. He had then decided to emigrate to Madinah. When the Quraysh came to hear of his intentions, they became very angry and tortured and imprisoned him. However, he finally managed to escape and arrived in Madinah. Unfortunately, Abu Baseer had been followed by two of the Quraysh who had come to arrest him and take him back to Makkah. The Prophet ﷺ prayed that Allah might protect Abu Baseer, because according to the terms of the treaty, he had to let him go with the two men.

Once again the hearts of the Muslims were very disturbed by this decision. A short while later, however, everybody was amazed to see Abu Baseer returning on a horse, but without his Quraysh guards. He explained that he had killed one of them and that the other had escaped. The other had, in fact, reached the Prophet first and refused to take Abu Baseer back because he feared for his life. Abu Baseer was hoping that this time the Prophet ﷺ would allow him to stay. Sadly, the Prophet ﷺ told him that he would not be allowed to live in Madinah because they had to honour the terms of the Treaty. His Quraysh guard no longer wanted Abu Baseer so he was released to go wherever he wanted. The Prophet ﷺ prayed that Allah would protect him and give him a way to survive.

It was some months later that a man from Makkah turned up in Madinah, wanting to see the Prophet ﷺ. At first, everyone thought that he might be a Muslim and warned him that he would not be allowed to stay in the city. He then explained that he had been sent by the Quraysh with a request that one of the conditions of the treaty should be changed. They wanted to permit any Muslims who wished to leave Makkah, to emigrate to Madinah!

The Prophet ﷺ was very surprised by this request. The man then told him that Abu Baseer and other Muslims refugees from Makkah, including Abu Jandal, were hiding in the desert. There were now seventy of them. Whenever, the Quraysh sent caravans across the desert to trade, these refugees would attack them. The citizens of Makkah were suffering human and financial losses. They were increasingly concerned that more and more Muslim refugees would join Abu Baseer and his friends. The Prophet ﷺ, of course, agreed to the request and, as a result, a very large number of Muslims emigrated to Madinah over the following months.

As agreed in the treaty, the following year, the Prophet ﷺ with many hundreds of Muslims made the journey to Makkah to perform the 'Umrah. With great misgivings, the Quraysh left the city for a period of three days. They felt that their own influence was weakening while Islam was growing more powerful by the day.

These fears were strengthened when looking down from the hills around Makkah, they watched the Prophet ﷺ and his companions perform the rites of the 'Umrah. The Prophet ﷺ was not given the key to the Ka'bah so he was not able to enter it as this was not a requirement of performing the 'Umrah. When at the Prophet's request, Bilal climbed on to the roof of the Ka'bah to call the adhan, the Quraysh were outraged. They could not believe their eyes when they saw this former black slave standing on the roof of the sacred structure and heard his strong, deep voice resounding through the city and beyond, echoing from one hill to another.

After three days had passed, the Muslims left Makkah to return to Madinah having completed the 'Umrah.

THE QURAYSH BREAK THE TREATY OF HUDAYBIYYAH

It was not long after the Muslims performed the 'Umrah, that news reached Madinah of fighting that had taken place in Makkah. A small number of Quraysh had joined the Bakr tribe in attacking the Bani Khuza'ah, allies of the Muslims. They had then together chased the Bani Khuza'ah into the haram around Makkah where they had killed some of them in the fighting.

A man called 'Amr managed to escape to Madinah and told the Prophet ﷺ what had happened there. Although only a few of Quraysh had been involved, this incident was very serious as it meant that they had violated one of the main terms of the treaty.

The leaders of Quraysh soon heard the news and, realising

that the treaty had been broken, they were very anxious to persuade the Prophet ﷺ to renew it. The Messenger ﷺ did not
respond immediately as he was waiting to receive Allah's guidance. However, when the Quraysh sent Abu Sufyan to Madinah
to ask the Prophet ﷺ to extend the time of the treaty, the Prophet ﷺ refused their request. In fact, everybody either treated
Abu Sufyan very coldly or with anger and disdain. Even his
daughter who was a devoted Muslim, could only ask him why
he had not entered Islam. His mission was obviously a complete
failure – all he could do was to return to Makkah empty-handed.

THE PROPHET AS A LEADER

Muhammad ﷺ had shown his qualities as a Prophet and Messenger from the time he first started to renew the ancient way of
Ibrahim. However, during the Hijrah he took an active part in the
planning of the battles, always endeavouring to have as few
casualties as possible and showed that he was an able military
leader. But whenever possible, he preferred to find a peaceful
way of settling conflicts and demonstrated that he was also a
skilful diplomat by the many peace treaties he arranged with
neighbouring tribes.

He looked beyond the boundaries of Arabia and sent letters
and ambassadors to the kings and heads of neighbouring countries calling on them to accept Islam. In response some of them
sent representatives to the Prophet ﷺ to find out more about
Islam and to try to strengthen the ties between them. The Prophet ﷺ always remained deeply grateful to the Negus, the King
of Abyssinia, for protecting some of the Muslims during the early
days of persecution and there existed a deep mutual respect
between the two men, and indeed the Negus had become a Muslim but had concealed it from his people. When later the Negus
sent a delegation to Madinah, the Prophet ﷺ insisted that they
be his personal guests.

THE CONQUEST OF MAKKAH 630 CE

Following the breaking of the Treaty of Hudaybiyyah and the
guidance that he received from Allah, the Prophet ﷺ sent a
message to all the Muslims in the area. He said that all those

who believed in Allah the One and in the Day of Judgement, should come to Madinah for the beginning of Ramadan.

Preparations for war began and people started flooding in from the surrounding regions with weapons, camels and horses. They set out on their journey as soon as the Prophet ﷺ gave the command but nobody except those closest to the Prophet ﷺ knew where they were going. It was the month of the Fast and the Prophet ﷺ allowed people not to fast or fast as they wished. When travelling, a Muslim may break his fast as long as he makes up the number of days that he has missed by fasting at another time. They finally reached Marr az-Zahran where they encamped. The Prophet ﷺ gave the command that everyone should stop fasting to gather their strength.

People were very curious as to what their destination was and whom they were going to attack. Makkah lay one to two days' march away. There were other places and tribes that were also within easy reach. But the Prophet ﷺ would not reveal his plans when people asked him. Instead he commanded every person in his army to light a campfire. There were ten thousand men in his army, so ten thousand campfires could be seen from the outskirts of Makkah. The town of Ta'if became uneasy and the inhabitants called on their allies to defend them. However, it was the Quraysh who were really worried because they knew that they had broken the truce. They held a big meeting at which they decided to send Abu Sufyan with two companions to try once again to talk to the Messenger of Allah ﷺ, and to persuade him to renew the Treaty of Hudaybiyyah.

As Abu Sufyan and his companions were making their way to the Prophet ﷺ they were met by al-'Abbas, the uncle of the Prophet who had just then emigrated to Madinah meeting the Messenger of Allah ﷺ and his army of almost ten thousand men on the way. He was on his way now to advise the leaders of Quraysh, for their own safety and survival, not to try to defend Makkah. He took Abu Sufyan and his two companions to the Prophet ﷺ. The two companions instantly became Muslims but Abu Sufyan could not bring himself to acknowledge Muhammad ﷺ as the Prophet of Allah. However, when next morning he saw the Muslims hurrying to prepare for their dawn prayers, he was deeply impressed. He saw the strong love that they had for the Prophet ☙ and the kind of loyalty that even Caesar was not given by his subjects. He finally decided to become a Muslim.

The Prophet ☙ paraded the various troops with their fine equipment in front of Abu Sufyan so that he could really witness the size and the quality of the army. Abu Sufyan could not have failed to be awed by all that he saw. He also remarked on the presence of some of the Prophet's former enemies who were now in the ranks of this army and who were so clearly devoted to him. The Prophet ☙ then sent Abu Sufyan back to Makkah with a message. He promised that all citizens of Makkah who stayed in their own or in Abu Sufyan's house or went to the Ka'bah would not be harmed. Seeing the enormous army, the inhabitants of Makkah – especially the Quraysh – realised that the time had come for their surrender and most remained obediently in their homes.

The Prophet formed the army into four divisions to each enter the Sacred City from a different direction. Riding on his camel, Qaswa at the head of one of the divisions, the Prophet ☙ entered Makkah solemnly reciting an ayah from the Qur'an:

"VERILY WE HAVE GRANTED YOU A CLEAR VICTORY"

(Qur'an 48:1)

The Messenger of Allah ☙ moved through the quiet, empty streets to the Ka'bah around which he rode seven times. Then repeating the ayah:

"THE TRUTH HAS COME AND FALSEHOOD HAS VANISHED"

(Qur'an 17: 81)

he pointed at each of the three hundred and sixty idols which stood in the courtyard and they each fell over. He asked for the key to the Ka'bah and, entering with Bilal, he instructed his companions to wash down the walls. Once the Sacred House was clean, he purified it by walking to each corner and reciting the shahadah:

"Laa ilaha illa'llah – There is no god except Allah"

He commanded Bilal to once again climb on to the roof of the Ka'bah to call the adhan. This was only the second time that the Muslim call to prayer was heard in the Sacred City of Makkah.

The first time had been during the 'Umrah. But this time the Muslims had come to reclaim the city. After the adhan the Prophet ﷺ prayed.

In the meantime, a little distance from the Ka'bah, the Quraysh gathered anxiously waiting to find out what their punishment might be. They were aware of the Prophet's reputation for compassion, but they also knew that he would have every right to punish them for the many years during which they had fought Islam and persecuted and tortured the Muslims. After praying, the Messenger of Allah ﷺ came out of the Ka'bah and faced them. His expression was serene. He first offered praises to Allah and then quoted the words from the Glorious Qur'an that the Prophet Yusuf (Joseph) ﷺ had spoken to his brothers:

"THIS DAY THERE WILL BE NO UPBRAIDING OF YOU NOR REPROACH. MAY ALLAH FORGIVE YOU, AND HE IS THE MOST MERCIFUL OF THE MERCIFUL."

However, he also told the Quraysh that Allah had taken away from the haughtiness of the time of ignorance and the veneration of ancestors, and reminded them that like everyone else, they were all descended from Adam. The Prophet ﷺ then allowed them to leave without punishment.

This was a supreme moment in the life of the Prophet Muhammad ﷺ. He could so easily have punished those who had attacked, tortured and killed the Muslims, among whom were members of his own family. He had every opportunity – and some would say right – to seek revenge. But at this moment he showed that he was truly a great and magnanimous person. His interest could not be in personal gain, power or revenge, but only in carrying out the Will of Allah the Almighty.

He ordered that all idols in Makkah were to be destroyed – indeed every household had at least one – and then he went to the hill of Safa where hundreds of his former enemies came to him to enter Islam.

Parties of Muslims were sent out to other pagan temples to destroy the idols and the whole area of Makkah was once again made sacred ground. Many of the Arabs saw that nothing terrible happened to those Muslims who destroyed the idols. This gave them the courage to become Muslims themselves.

They were also deeply impressed by the mercy and compassion that the Prophet ﷺ had shown them. Through this act of forgiving his enemies he, no doubt, won more hearts for Islam, than he could ever have done through battle.

THE PROPHET'S FAREWELL HAJJ AND LAST KHUTBAH

When the Prophet ﷺ emigrated to Madinah, he had left two houses in Makkah but he never claimed them back. In fact, while he was in Makkah he had his tent erected outside the Sacred City and did not stay in anybody's home. He preferred to go back to Madinah which had become his home, and to the people who had given him and the Muhajirun protection and succour. The Ansar were the people who had suffered side by side with him and the Muslim emigrants, and they had become his family.

It was two years later that he returned to Makkah to undertake the Greater Pilgrimage called the Hajj. He was accompanied by a large crowd of people. There were people of Makkah and Madinah and from other tribes as well as other areas. After completing the Hajj he called the crowds together and spoke to them from the Mount of Mercy on the Plain of 'Arafat. This was called his Last Khutbah, and this Hajj was called 'The Farewell Pilgrimage'.

It must have been a very moving sight to see the thousands of people collected there standing with their faces turned towards the Messenger of Allah ﷺ. They were listening intently. For most of them this would be the last time they would ever see him – although at the time they probably did not realise this. The crowds were so large that "criers" had to be used to repeat the Prophet's words to those who were standing at the furthest edges of the crowds and who, therefore, could not hear him.

The Prophet ﷺ told them that he might not be with them for long and reminded them of everything he had taught them. He warned them to remember and follow the guidance that he had given them. He asked them whether he had delivered Allah's message, to which they all, in one voice replied, that he had. In response he cried 'Witness, O Allah!'.

EXCERPTS FROM THE FAREWELL KHUTBAH

"O People, lend me an attentive ear, for I do know not whether, after this year, I shall ever be amongst you again. Therefore, listen to what I am saying to you very carefully, and take these words to those who could not be present here today... Just as you regard this month, this day, this city as sacred, so regard the life and property of every Muslim as a sacred trust. Hurt no one so that no one may hurt you. Remember you will indeed meet your Lord, and that he will indeed reckon your deeds...

"It is true that you have certain rights with regard to your women, but they also have rights over you...they are your partners and committed helpers... Worship Allah, do your five daily Salah (prayers), fast during the month of Ramadan, and give your wealth in Zakat. Perform Hajj if you are able to...

"...Every Muslim is the brother of another Muslim.... Nobody has superiority over another except by taqwa (fearful awareness of Allah) and good deeds... No Arab is superior to a non-Arab and no non-Arab is superior to an Arab. No dark-skinned person is superior to a white person and no white person is superior to a dark-skinned person...

"Remember, one day you will appear before Allah and answer for your actions. So beware, do not stray from the path of right action after I am gone... No prophet will come after me and no new faith will be born... I leave behind me two things, the Qur'an and my example – the Sunnah, and if you follow these you will never go astray... All those who listen to me shall pass on my words to others, and those to others again; and may the last ones understand my words better than those who listen to me directly...

"Be my witness, O Allah, that I have conveyed Your message to Your people!"

He never returned to Makkah and eighty days later died in Madinah⁓ .

THE ILLNESS AND DEATH OF THE PROPHET

When the Prophet ﷺ fell ill, he said that it was the result of the poison left in his body when some years before somebody had tried to kill him. As he became weaker during his illness, he told Abu Bakr to lead the prayers.

The living quarters of his family opened out on to the mosque, and each wife had her own quarters. The Prophet ﷺ had always stayed one day with each wife in turn and did not have his own apartment. However, during the last days of his illness which lasted thirteen days, his wives agreed that he should stay with A'ishah ﵂ .

On the morning of the seventh of June 732 CE, after the Fajr (Dawn) prayers, with a tremendous effort he made his way to the mosque. The Muslims were delighted to see him. Many remarked on how radiant he looked. They thought he was getting better. But he felt death close and may have been apprehensive because he knew that there would be disagreements after he had died. He spoke about this and again reminded people to follow the guidance he had brought them. He then cried loudly: "Allah is my witness that you cannot reproach me. Truly, I have allowed what the Qur'an allows and forbidden what the Qur'an forbids". He returned to A'ishah's quarters and died at about noon with his head in her lap. A'ishah, with Khadijah's daughter, Fatimah, and Fatimah's husband, Ali ﵂ are said to have witnessed the arrival of both the angel Jibril and the Angel of Death.

ABU BAKR COMFORTS THE COMPANIONS

The community was profoundly shocked when they heard that their beloved Prophet ﷺ had died, and did not want to believe the terrible news. When reports of this reached Abu Bakr, he hurried back to A'ishah's quarters where he saw for himself, that his beloved ﵂ had indeed passed away. Weeping, he entered the mosque and calmed the Companions. Then he spoke quietly: "If it was Muhammad whom you worshipped, he is dead. But if you are servants of Allah, indeed He is the Ever Living One, the Eternal". He comforted them and reminded them of the gift of the Qur'an. He also recited a few ayat of the Qur'an to remind them that Allah had told them that the Prophet ﷺ was a man – a Messenger of Allah. One day he would die, like previous messengers. Abu Bakr accepted with great humility the Companions' request that he should become their leader, and became the first Caliph or Successor of the Messenger of Allah .

The Messenger once said that a Prophet of Allah should be buried in the same spot where he died. So the Prophet's body was washed in the ritual way after which all the inhabitants of Madinah came to pray over it. First the men came, then the women followed by the children. When all had been able to pray and say their own farewells to the Prophet they buried his body in a grave in A'ishah's quarters.

There was much weeping, especially among those who had been closest to the Prophet . They all knew that the Prophet had gone to his Lord and would be there in the Divine Presence awaiting them when they died and were raised up on the Last Day – indeed this is what the Prophet had promised them. Although they tried to console each other, they all felt the loss very deeply. Bilal's legs collapsed under him and he was not able to go up to the roof without help. When he did eventually reach the roof with assistance, his overwhelming grief made it impossible for him to call the adhan. It is said that only twice after that did he call the adhan again. He could not even bear to remain in Madinah, and moved to Syria.

The mosque in Madinah has been enlarged over the centuries and now includes in it the Prophet's tomb.

The Prophet Muhammad was, without doubt, the greatest of the Messengers of Allah and the most remarkable man in history. From a childhood watching sheep, he became a successful trader until his marriage to Khadijah. Despite a very happy marriage, his restless soul would take him to the mountain cave where he would immerse himself in prayer and meditation. Then one day, the angel Jibril visited him and his life changed dramatically. This change brought him prophethood and the many roles he eventually played in the service of Allah the One the Almighty.

It was through Allah's guidance, that this man became the greatest of all spiritual leaders, a man who called the emperors of the Byzantine, Persian and Abyssinian Empires to Islam, a military commander who achieved astonishing conquests with remarkably little loss of life and whose former enemies came to love him as passionately as they had once hated him, the leader of a community dealing with all the minute matters of everyday governance, a man whose behaviour made the revelation of the Qur'an into a tangible living model, and a father to all Muslims. He never distanced himself from his people. No matter how he suffered, he would still manage to extend a hand to somebody he felt was needier than himself. His compassion, love, patience and understanding had no match. His Ummah are utterly devoted to him and they love him above all others. The loss and desolation the Companions must have experienced when the Prophet ﷺ died is something that would be too overwhelming to imagine.

Some years later, Bilal ؓ returned to Madinah to visit the Prophet's grave. The Prophet's grandsons, Hasan and Hussain ؓ , pleaded with him to call the adhan just once. Bilal could not refuse. As his voice once again resounded over the city, men and women came into the street weeping, recalling the time when their beloved Messenger ﷺ was still with them.

Chapter 4: The Legacy of the Prophet Muhammad

QUOTATIONS FROM THE HADITH

Here are a few sayings of the Prophet Muhammad ﷺ :

"He who is not grateful to men, is not grateful to Allah."

"Kindness adorns everything, while harshness disgraces everything."

"Allah has no mercy on him who is not kind to people."

"A soft heart is near Allah, while a hard heart is remote from Him."

"He who is devoid of all kindness is devoid of all good."

"The key to Paradise is love for the poor."

"Feed the hungry, visit the sick and free the captive."

"Be in the world as though you were a stranger or a wayfarer."

"Whosoever removes a worldly grief from a believer, Allah will remove from him one of the griefs on the Day of Judgement."

"Each person's every joint must perform a sadaqah every day the sun comes up: to act justly between two people is a sadaqah; to help a man with his horse, lifting him on to it or hoisting up his belongings on to it is a sadaqah; a good word is a sadaqah; every step you take to prayers (i.e. on the way to the mosque) is a sadaqah; and removing a harmful thing from the road is a sadaqah."

"Purity is half of faith... Prayer is light. Sadaqah is a proof; patience is illumination; and the Qur'an is an argument for or against you. Everyone starts his day and is a vendor of his soul, either freeing it or bringing about its ruin."

"People are Allah's family. Therefore the dearest to Allah is the person who is kind to His family."

"The pleasure of Allah is in the pleasure of the father, and

the displeasure of Allah is in the displeasure of the father."
"...Paradise is beneath her (a mother's) feet."
"When an obedient child looks at his parents with a kind look, Allah writes for him (the credit equal to) one accepted Pilgrimage for every look."

THE INFLUENCE OF THE PROPHET AND ISLAM ON EVERY FACET OF HUMAN LIFE

Michael H. Hart in his book THE 100 – A RANKING OF THE MOST INFLUENTIAL PERSONS IN HISTORY (1978) wrote that his choice of Muhammad ﷺ to lead the list of the world's most influential persons might surprise some readers and may be questioned by others, but that he regarded the Messenger of Allah ﷺ as the only man in history who was supremely successful on both the spiritual and worldly levels.

A century earlier, John William Draper, in volume one of his A HISTORY OF THE INTELLECTUAL DEVELOPMENT OF EUROPE, wrote: "Four years after the death of Justinian, A.D. 569, was born in Makkah, in Arabia, the man who, of all men, has exercised the greatest influence upon the human race."

By his own example the Prophet ﷺ demonstrated how Muslims should live. Here are a few main areas of his work in the social and governmental fields that express what he stood for.

HUMAN RIGHTS AND DUTIES

He greatly improved the conditions of slaves and encouraged people to give their slaves their freedom if they were ready for it. Slaves can be freed in expiation for a number of wrong actions of their owners, and there are a number of contractual ways in which slaves may attain freedom, including being set free on their master's death or writing a contract to purchase their freedom. If people do have slaves, they are to treat them like members of the family. They are to be given the same food and the same clothes as their masters wear, and are not to be beaten unnecessarily. Burdensome work is to be shared by the slave and master.

He told people that nobody was any better than anybody else merely because of his genealogy or pedigree, but only through taqwa – fearful awareness of Allah and right action. An Arab is not necessarily better than a non-Arab. There should be no discrimination based on colour, race, tribe or caste. In the eyes of Allah, it is not important what colour skin a person has, or what position he may hold. Allah will only judge a person on how he lives his life, by his submission to the Will of Allah and his obedience to the Messenger and his successors and the people in authority, his acts of worship, sadaqah and his struggling in jihad.

Arnold Toynbee, one of the most famous historians of this century, remarked that the extinction of race consciousness among Muslims is one of the outstanding achievements of Islam, and that in the world today there is 'a crying need for the propagation of this Islamic virtue'.

MARRIAGE AND WOMEN'S RIGHTS

Marriage is a key part of the shari'ah of Islam. It is every Muslim's duty to marry once they reach maturity if they are able. Marriage is very important, and therefore, men and women must come to it in a pure state. Men and women are partners to each other. They each have certain duties to each other and certain responsibilities. Women were given dignity and rights which many women in the West did not achieve until the twentieth century. These include the right not to marry somebody they do not like, the right to divorce, to receive maintenance for their children if divorced, to inherit, to own property and to engage in trade.

LAW

The Law is there to give protection to every Muslim – man, woman or child, from injustice or wrongdoing. The judgements were developed according to the Qur'an. In law, each party must be given a fair hearing and the sentence must be fair and just. According to the Charter of Madinah drawn up by the Prophet ﷺ about a year after he had moved there, non-Muslims – in this case the Jews – were given a clear contract of their contractual rights and obligations vis a vis the Muslims. However, this document is not a legal model for Muslims' dealings with non-Muslims, for that has to be based on the model developed by the

Khulafa ar-Rashidun after the death of the Messenger of Allah ﷺ which they founded on their profound knowledge of the Qur'an and the Sunnah. That grants a certain inferior status to the Jews and Christians under Muslim governance as long as they pay the jizyah and observe a very well-defined code of behaviour, such as not making any obvious display of their acts of worship, or of drinking alcohol in public, and not dressing as the Muslims do, etc.

MUSLIM GOVERNANCE

Muslim governance must be based on the Noble Book of Allah and the Sunnah of the Messenger of Allah ﷺ and of the Khalifahs who took the right way after him﷽ , and it must be tempered with fairness, justice and compassion. The Prophet ﷺ created a model society, where every person with knowledge or experience has a right and even a duty to speak their mind but nobody is above the law. The main administrators must have a knowledge of the Qur'an and Sunnah, and they also have to be known for their honesty and fair-dealing.

There is a Treasury or Community Chest created to look after the affairs of the community. A part of that fund is the zakat which can be used for the needs of the poor, travellers, the disabled and people who have recently come to Islam. This is a welfare society which yet encourages people to be independent and work rather than beg. There is a generous freedom within the broad parameters of what is permitted by Allah in the Qur'an.

When Muslims took over a city or area, they were given strict instructions that homes were not to be destroyed, nor fruit trees nor people's livelihoods, churches, monasteries and revered buildings. Women, children, invalids in bed, priests and religious leaders, and men who are not fighting are also not to be harmed. There is to be no oppression and no meddling in people's lives.

Islam is never to be spread by compulsion. In his dealings and negotiations with heads of neighbouring countries, the Prophet ﷺ demonstrated how these should be carried out. He would tell them about Islam in a letter, and invite them to submit, or he would send a representative to them to carry the message of Islam. On several occasions he was host to foreign delegations and there were also exchanges of gifts between himself and the heads of these countries. However, in obedience to his last commands and some of the last revealed ayat of the Qur'an the Companions waged war on the Byzantines and the Persians, vigorously demanding of them that they should either submit in Islam, accept to live under Islamic governance or fight. If they fought and then the Muslims conquered them, the Muslims had the choice of enslaving them, killing them, or drawing up the contract of the Dhimmah with them which includes their jizyah payment, but they are not allowed to forcibly convert the People of the Book to Islam.

Non-Muslims have to pay a small tax which Allah, exalted is He, indicates in the Qur'an is to mark their humiliation. It may be used to cover the expenses of defending the city and looking after it and for other matters. They are not allowed to take part in fighting with the Muslims. Whereas it is the duty of every able-bodied adult male Muslim to fight for the establishment of Islam and in the defence of the Muslims.

EDUCATION, SCIENCE TECHNOLOGY AND CRAFTS

"He who seeks a road to knowledge, Allah paves for him a road to the Garden", the Prophet ﷺ is said to have commented. This reflects the great importance that Islam places on education and learning. The Noble Qur'an encourages people to observe and study the world around them and this gave enormous impetus to the development of science and the arts.

In Islam education is regarded very highly. It is the duty of every Muslim – male and female – to seek knowledge, specifically knowledge of those matters of the way of Islam which are of immediate importance such as knowledge of the rules of trade for a man who is a trader, for if he does not know them he will become involved in usury without meaning to. Similarly, it is obligatory for a man or woman to know everything that is needed to perform the prayer and to understand it, and when Ramadan comes around it is obligatory to know the limits of fasting. So, as it is obligatory to seek really useful knowledge, it is not allowed to seek useless knowledge while neglecting vital knowledge. Spurred on by the Prophet's interest in and support of craftsmen and education, there was a great flowering of the sciences and arts in the Muslim Ummah.

The battles initially pushed artisans in the workshops of Madinah to study ways of forging strong steel for swords. With time they developed and perfected the technology of crucible steel forging that they had learnt from India, and even today some of the swords they made are still in excellent condition with smooth sharp blades. Damascus and Toledo were famous in the Middle Ages for the workmanship and quality of their blades. Their skills in metallurgy also developed in the art of inlaying gold and silver pieces into brass and bronze.

Surgery and medicine were studied to heal the wounded. After the battle of Uhud, the Prophet ﷺ set up a medical tent in the precincts of the mosque. This was supervised by a female Muslim surgeon, Rafaida. The Prophet ﷺ also assisted with the care of the patients. The cleanliness stipulated by the Qur'an and the Sunnah helped to decrease disease greatly, and created a greater awareness of health-care, as did the awareness of a pure diet, fasting Ramadan and not eating and drinking to excess. During the years in Madinah, the Prophet ﷺ was frequently visited by foreign delegations, and from them A'ishah learnt ways of curing many ailments. The Prophet ﷺ urged her to teach others what she knew.

In the centuries after the Prophet's death, Muslim doctors were foremost in their fields of specialisation. Even before western doctors understood contagion, Arab doctors were already dividing wards according to the different diseases. Many of the works that they wrote and compiled served European medical schools until the seventeenth century.

As Islam spread, there was a general growth in all areas of life. The meeting of people from different countries meant that there was an exchange of knowledge. More and more mosques were built and architecture flourished. Travel meant a greater study of geography and astronomy.

Muslims studied the work and achievements of the Chinese, Indians and Greeks. They also observed the world around them and made great strides in the development of both science and the arts which was expressed in the great flowering of Islamic civilisation. There were many eminent Muslims in later years who became famous in the fields of medicine, surgery, chemistry, mathematics, botany, veterinary science, astronomy, optics, geography, cartography, physics, irrigation, architecture, navigation, philosophy and so on. For instance, in the middle of the eighth century CE, Jabir ibn Hayyan laid down the rules for performing experiments in chemistry which are valid even today.

In a lecture called MANKIND'S DEBT TO THE PROPHET MUHAMMAD ﷺ given in 1989, S. Abul Hasan Ali Nadwi describes how through the various developments in science, Muslims developed a new method of thinking where deductive logic was replaced by a process of observation and experiment followed by inductive logic. This new method spread to the rest of Europe via Muslim Spain and is the foundation of all modern science and technology.

One outstanding feature of the developments in science and technology undertaken by the Muslims was that it never harmed the environment. This is in accordance with what is prescribed in the Noble Qur'an. Although people did have the skills to develop complicated machinery, they did not do this as they feared the results could be detrimental to the environment. The extent of their technological skills and potential can be seen in the complicated small-scale mechanisms they built for various princes, which were the equivalent of executive toys in our times.

This intense activity and development occurred not only in the realms of science and technology but also in philosophy and the arts: textile weaving of silk, damask linen, wool and cotton, glass-making, ceramics and glazed tiles with the most amazing colours and designs, rugs of extraordinary beauty, music, literature and poetry; the making of books with leather bindings and manuscript illuminations, and of course, the most exquisite calligraphy glorifying Allah which was used to decorate everything from buildings to fabrics.

SOME OF THE THINGS THAT MAKE A PERSON A MUSLIM

There are some things that every Muslim must do and these things are known as the Five Pillars of Islam. In addition, there are things that a Muslim is required to believe in. In both the Qur'an and the Sunnah there is guidance for Muslims as to how they should behave and what is recommended and what is forbidden. The Prophet's life is full of beautiful examples for Muslims to follow.

THE FIVE PILLARS OF ISLAM

The five Pillars of Islam (Arkan al-Islam) are the duty of every Muslim to perform. These are:

The shahadah:

To witness: Ash-hadu al'laa ilaha illa'llah, wa ash-hadu anna Muhammadar-rasulu'llah.

This means: "I bear witness that there is no god except Allah, and that Muhammad is the Messenger of Allah." When somebody has decided to become a Muslim, these are the words they have to repeat in front of Muslim witnesses.

These words are the basis of everything else in Islam, and the following 'pillars' are the putting into practice of the shahadah.

To perform the Salah (the five daily prayers) regularly.

These are:

The Fajr prayers performed at dawn and up until before sunrise.

The Dhuhr prayers performed just after midday when the sun has passed its highest point.

The 'Asr prayers performed when the sun has just passed the halfway mark between the highest point and sunset.

The Maghrib prayers performed after sunset.

The 'Isha prayers which are performed once the redness has gone from the sky.

A Muslim performs these prayers (salah) which contain certain words and actions. This is why we talk about Muslims 'doing' or 'performing' these prayers, rather than 'saying' them.

There are other prayers – supplications – that can be said without accompanying actions. These prayers are called in Arabic Du'a. Muslims are also encouraged to remember Allah all through the day and night and we will often repeat words to remember, glorify and praise Him. Sometimes we use a tasbih (beads) to help us count the number of times we repeat the words.

To give Zakah, a proportion of wealth – gold and silver, cattle, crops, the produce of mines, and goods kept for sale – to be used for helping the poor and needy. It is laid down that 2.5 per cent of a person's savings or unused wealth over the level known as the nisab, which he or she has left untouched for a year, has to be taken by the Amir every year and distributed among eight categories including the poor, the extremely needy, travellers, in the way of Allah, for debtors, and to free slaves.

To observe the Fast of Ramadan. (See section on Ramadan)

To perform the Hajj or pilgrimage to Makkah, for those who are able and have the means to do so.

The Muslim also needs to recognise and believe in:

Allah, the One God

His Mala'ikah (Angels)

His revealed Books. There are said to have been 104 altogether including the Tawrah and Zabur (Psalms of the Prophet Dawud﷽) and the Injil revealed to 'Isa﷽ , and the Qur'an. None of these 104 books any longer exist in clear unaltered form except for the Qur'an. Muslims should respect these other revelations. Through the centuries, parts of the texts of the earlier books were lost or altered so that they are no longer as they were originally. Because of this, and through the grace of Allah Who guaranteed to preserve the Qur'an, Muslims have been very careful never to change even one word of the Qur'an. The Qur'an contains among its vast reservoir of wisdom and illumination the truths revealed in all the previous Books, and it corrects much that was altered in the earlier revelations.

His Prophets and Messengers. These include the prophets who are mentioned in the Old Testament as well as 'Isa﷽ . 'Isa and his mother, Maryam (Mary), are mentioned often in the Qur'an. They are regarded as very special and devoted people. In fact, Maryam is mentioned more times in the Qur'an than in the New Testament. Muhammad ﷺ is the last in the line of the Prophets, he is the Seal of all the Prophets, the Beloved of Allah and the one who will intercede for the believers on the Last Day when even the other Prophets will be occupied with their own accounts.

The Last Day, the Day of Accounting or the Yawm ad-Din. During their life on earth, people's actions and deeds are recorded by angels. After the day the world ends and after the resurrection from the graves, and on a day whose measure is said to be a thousand years, their deeds and actions will be displayed and weighed by Allah. Those who have had a true tawhid and worshipped Him and done good deeds will be rewarded with the joys and beauty of the Garden or the Jannah. People who have covered over the true nature of tawhid and turned away from Allah and lived evil lives will be punished in the fire of Jahannam

A MUSLIM'S DIET

The Qur'an gives Muslims certain rules about diet. These judgements, all other judgements of Islam, the Muslims obey unquestioningly but they understand that a part of the wisdom in them is that they are to help Muslims be healthy and to look after their bodies. Muslims may never do anything to harm themselves, or anybody else – except of course in war or the execution of punishments for contravention of the legal limits. But even then they are not permitted to use any force that is not absolutely necessary. The following are haram (forbidden) for a Muslim:

PORK IN ANY FORM

Meat that is not halal (not killed according to the guidance of the Noble Qur'an and the practice of the Sunnah).

Animals that are killed for meat must be healthy. To avoid causing them pain they should be comforted and then slaughtered according to the guidance of the Sunnah. Meat that is from animals killed in this way, as well as other foods that Muslims are permitted to eat, are called halal.

Blood (a consequence of this is that meat ought to be washed and cooked well).

ALCOHOL AND NARCOTIC DRUGS

When people drink alcohol and take narcotic drugs they begin to lose control of themselves and also their minds. In this state it is easy to forget Allah which is the worst and most serious of all disasters which no other catastrophe could equal and from which all other wrong actions stem, and to do silly or bad things. Apart from that, alcohol and drugs are harmful to the health.

The words haram and halal are also used for anything that a Muslim is or is not allowed to do – see next section.

A MUSLIM'S BEHAVIOUR

True Muslims should be known by their courtesy, for courtesy follows on from awareness of the presence of Allah and of His watchfulness. All of the following qualities of character and behaviour stem from the same source:

They should dress modestly, and be kind and gentle to others. They should respect other people – especially their parents and older people. A Muslim must perform his prayers regularly but if he lives selfishly and does not care for those around him there is some contradiction in his understanding. It is a Muslim's duty to protect the weak and fight for justice in society, and that can only ever be done by establishing the governance of Islam and the rule of the shari'ah.

A Muslim should have qualities such as honesty, courage, purity, loyalty, truthfulness, obedience to the leaders of the Muslims, the people of knowledge, his parents and teachers, humility, kindness, and care for others. Muslims should not lie, gossip, backbite, be cruel or uncaring.

Muslims should be kind to animals. A wrongdoing woman – reputedly a prostitute – once gave water to a dog that was dying of thirst. The Prophet ﷺ said that Allah had forgiven all her wrong actions because of this kind act.

Marriage is regarded as something very important in Islam and both the man and woman should come to their wedding in a clean and pure state. Therefore, men and women are not allowed to sleep with each other until they are married. Once married, they are forbidden to have affairs outside their marriage. Monogamy is a Sunnah of the Jews and Christians and polygamy the sunnah of the Messenger of Allah ﷺ. No Muslim man has any excuse for having affairs; he is permitted to propose to and marry such women as he feels attracted to and is capable of supporting, up to the number of four.

The Qur'an speaks frequently of purity – the importance of physical and spiritual cleanliness. This is not a compulsive fear of dirt and obsession with being permanently and unnaturally clean. The symbolism of taking wudu or ablutions before doing the salah is quite clear: that becoming dirty is an ordinary part of life, and the Muslim, accepting that, washes the dirt of the world off, both inwardly and outwardly before the prayer. It is also seen in the ghusl or ritual bath that men and women must take before going to the mosque on Friday and after intercourse. Although the washing or bathing is a physical cleaning of the body, it has an inward effect when done with that consciousness and is a purification of the mind and the heart.

The Prophet ﷺ himself was very particular about cleanliness and, for example, would regularly clean his teeth and wash his mouth. Even on his deathbed, he asked to use a tooth-stick. This outward act is an indication of his inner condition of always turning to Allah from even the finest and subtlest of distractions.

14th-century mausoleum
of Sultan Hasan, Cairo

Part Two: The Muslim Festivals

EIDU'L-FITR AND EIDU'L-ADHA

'Eid' means 'recurring happiness' or 'festivity'. Eidu'l-Fitr is the 'Festival of Breaking (the Fast)'. It marks the end of the fast of the month of Ramadan.

Eidu'l-Adha (The Festival of the Sacrifice) falls on the tenth day of the Muslim month of Dhu'l-Hijjah. It takes place at the end of the Hajj (pilgrimage to Makkah).

Although these two festivals celebrate different events, they are in fact, similar because they each follow a period of hardship and self-denial. It is only possible to understand why these festivals are important when you also understand what preceded them.

Chapter 1: Ramadan and Eidu'l-Fitr

WHAT IS THE FAST OF RAMADAN?

In the Qur'an, the month of Ramadan is described as, 'that in which the Qur'an was revealed as a guidance for people'. The ayah goes on to explain who should fast, and who is allowed to not fast. Allah, glorious and exalted is He, then explains that

"ALLAH DESIRES EASE FOR YOU AND HE DOES NOT DESIRE HARDSHIP FOR YOU, AND (HE DESIRES) THAT YOU COMPLETE THE PRESCRIBED PERIOD (OF THE FAST) AND MAGNIFY ALLAH FOR HIS GUIDANCE TO YOU; AND THAT YOU MAY BE GRATEFUL".

(Qur'an 2: 185)

Ramadan is the ninth month of the Muslim calendar when all Muslims – with a few exceptions – have to fast during the hours of daylight. The first day of the fast is authorised by the Amir who has authenticated a sighting of the new moon. This is a very important moment when people often gather outside with great excitement. Each person hopes to be the first to see it. The lunar month can be twenty-nine or thirty days long, so they look for the new moon on the twenty-ninth day of Sha'ban, which is the month before Ramadan. If on the first evening the Amir is not satisfied that the new moon has been seen, Ramadan will begin on the following evening.

Once everyone knows that the month of Ramadan has started, they begin the preparations.

Early in the morning, each family gets up before dawn to eat a meal. It is dark and sometimes it is very difficult to get up, so parents try to encourage the children so that they don't miss their suhur or breakfast. After eating on the first morning they resolve on their intention to fast that month 'for the sake of Allah', and each day people similarly renew their intention to fast that day. From this moment their fast begins. They then perform their Fajr prayers.

During the day they must not eat, drink, have sexual relations or smoke. Even more important – they must try not to get angry or think bad thoughts, because this would also cancel out any good things they might receive from Allah through fasting. Many people find that because they are fasting they lose their tempers more quickly. So one of the first things that the fast teaches is self-control and patience.

The moment to break fast arrives as soon as the sun sets. Those who are fasting gather together and usually break their fast with a date and a glass of water. Sometimes they might have other snacks as well. The meal that you break fast with is called iftar.

After their Maghrib prayers, they sit down to eat a proper meal. The ritual of breaking the fast with dates is said to go back to the time when the Prophet 'Isa ﷵ was a baby, when he and his parents were fleeing to Egypt. On the journey they had nothing to eat. The first food that they were able to find was dates. So the baby 'Isa broke his fast with dates. Later, the Prophet Muhammad ﷺ also broke his fast with dates, and in this way it became a custom. When fasting it is very important to eat healthy food so that you will have strength to fast the next day. Sometimes people cook enormous meals and this can mean throwing food away if it is not all eaten. Food should never be wasted – especially during Ramadan. The Prophet ﷺ also advised that it is better never to eat too much.

After their meal many Muslims go to the mosque to do the Tarawih prayers after the night prayers called 'Isha. Tarawih are special prayers which are done every night at the mosque only during Ramadan. Sometimes people do them at home. During the prayers, many people will try to complete the reading of the whole Qur'an at least once in that month. For the twenty-nine or thirty days of the fast, Muslims will repeat this routine each day.

A few people are excused from fasting. Children under the age of puberty – though many start fasting much younger. They usually start by fasting just half a day. As they grow older they fast for longer periods, until they are able to complete the whole month. Women who have their periods or who have just given birth do not fast. If they are pregnant or breast-feeding they do not have to fast if they fear for the baby's health. The sick, the old and the traveller, are also excused from fasting. In all cases when people are not able to fast, they have to fast the number of days they have missed, at some other time. If they are not able to do this because of bad health, for instance, they must feed a poor person for the same number of days. This is only if they can afford it.

WHY MUSLIMS FAST

In the Qur'an it is written that the fast is not intended to be a burden for Muslims because it brings them many benefits. We know that fasting cleanses the body and clears the mind. By learning to be patient and suffering hunger and thirst, Muslims can feel how it must be to be poor and to have nothing to eat and drink. Fasting can also make Muslims strong and courageous when facing difficulties in their lives. The lack of food can make them feel weak physically, but Muslims often find that this helps them to focus on their lives and become more aware of their mistakes. As a result of this, they ask for Allah's forgiveness and pray for His blessing. Many feel that the fast makes their feelings calm and clean. By the end of the fast they feel renewed.

In Islam there are certain times when Muslims are reminded that although they may be important people in their work, they are all just human beings and creatures of Allah. The differences between races and between the rich and poor, disappear when the whole Ummah all over the world are united in doing the same activity. This happens at the mosque especially when Muslims meet for Friday prayers, and when there are big festivals. It also happens during Ramadan when rich and poor alike suffer hunger pangs. The fast of Ramadan is a very ancient practice and predates the Prophet Muhammad ﷺ – in fact, it is believed to date from the time of the Prophet Ibrahim ﷺ .

LAILATU'L-QADR

Ramadan is important because it was during this month that the Holy Qur'an was first received. The night when the Angel Jibril first came to the Prophet Muhammad ﷺ to bring him the divine message, is called 'Lailatu'l Qadr' – 'The Night of Power' or the 'Night of Decree'. It is said to fall on one of the last ten nights of the fast. It is the most important night for those who are fasting. It is not known exactly which night of Ramadan it is, but it is believed to be on one of the odd nights – twenty-first, twenty-third, twenty-fifth, twenty-seventh, or twenty-ninth. Many people believe that it is the twenty-seventh night.

On this night people who fast, hope to receive illumination or something special from Allah. This might take the form of a change in their character and understanding, guidance or the beginnings of a change in their lives. For this reason, Muslims will often stay up all night to pray on these special nights. In the Qur'an the Night of Power is described in the surah al-Qadr, as follows:

In the Name of Allah, the Most Beneficent, the Most Merciful
Surely We have revealed the Qur'an on the Night of Al-Qadr;
And what would make you know what is the Night of Al-Qadr?
The Night of Al-Qadr is better than a thousand months;
The angels and the Spirit (Jibril) descend in it
by their Lords' permission, with every decree.
Peace it is until the break of dawn.

(The Qur'an 97: 1-5)

When a whole family is fasting, the atmosphere at home often becomes very peaceful and calm. Nobody wants to spoil things by quarrelling and losing their tempers. During the last ten days, if they can, devoted Muslims will also spend much of their time praying and reciting the Qur'an at the mosque or alone at home.

THE MONTH COMES TO AN END

As the month draws to a close, there is once again great excitement. On the twenty-ninth evening people go to look for the new moon. If the Amir is not satisfied that it has been seen, the fast must continue for one more day and end after thirty days have been completed. Once it is known that the fast must end, the Amir will announce this in the mosque. It is forbidden to fast on Eidu'l-Fitr or Eidu'l-Adha (the latter is three days).

If someone has done the fast sincerely, he will usually feel great compassion for others and will have a strong desire to help the deprived or the disadvantaged. This is expressed through the Zakat al-Fitr, which is an amount of grain or food, which each person must give to someone who is needy. This is best done on the day of the Eid before the prayer of the Eid, so that the poor can celebrate Eidu'l-Fitr. No one must be left out on this day. Nearly everyone in the Ummah must give 'Fitr' because it is obligatory for whoever has more food than their requirements for one day. Parents will give on behalf of their young children and whoever they are responsible for maintaining.

EIDU'L- FITR

Although they may have a feeling of gladness that they have completed the fast, Muslims also feel a little sad when Ramadan is over. There is something special about the fast – it is a time of barakah, of special grace and blessings. Many devoted Muslims feel inwardly cleansed through fasting and they also feel reborn. But now it is time to rejoice.

NEW CLOTHES ARE A SYMBOL OF FEELING NEW AFTER THE FAST

Some do not sleep the night the fast ends – the beginning of Eidu'l-Fitr. They sit and pray, waiting for the dawning of the new day and new month. The musalla where the Eid prayer should properly be prayed is a piece of land outside the town or city where all the people of the town from all the different mosques will gather. In the morning everyone goes to the musalla in their best clothes. If they can afford it they wear new clothes. This is a symbol of inner renewal after the fast. The children especially are beautifully dressed and everyone is in a festive mood.

EIDU'L-FITR PRAYERS

There are special prayers held at the musalla in the morning. These are different from the usual prayers (salah) and different also from the Friday congregational prayers. They repeat many times the words 'Allahu Akbar' – Allah is the Most Great. Before and after the prayers, and through the day, people will chant the Takbir. This is a remembrance of Allah which is sung praising Allah and praying for the Prophet Muhammad ﷺ and his family and companions. The first part of this remembrance dates back to the time of the Prophet Ibrahim ﷺ :

"Allah is the Most Great, Allah is the Most Great
Allah is the Most Great.
There is no one worthy of worship except Allah
Allah is the Most Great, Allah is the Most Great
All praise is due to Allah."

Eidu'l-Fitr is a day when parents, children and friends ask forgiveness of each other, and thank Allah for all His Blessings. It is a day when Muslims can make a new start.

SHARING IN ISLAM

During his life, the Prophet Muhammad ﷺ tried to help Muslims to understand how important it is to be part of the community. In doing the fast and then celebrating Eidu'l-Fitr, people are drawn together, especially when they gather at the musalla or mosque. A symbol of the sharing is that during the fast, families will often send food to their neighbours to break fast with, or they invite each to share the breaking of the fast in their houses, or they invite strangers and travellers home to eat – this way they can all experience the barakah of the fast together. Again, during Eidu'l-Fitr, it is very important to share and enjoy food together.

AFTER FASTING COMES REMEMBRANCE OF ALLAH AND FEASTING

In Islam, you can find contrasts that constantly run through the religion. After a month of fasting and self-denial, Eidu'l-Fitr must be celebrated with remembrance of Allah, abundance and enjoyment. So after the prayers at the mosque are over, people greet each other with the words 'Eid Mubarak' (Blessings of Eid). The day passes in visiting families and friends and when the five prayers are done Allah is remembered. Everywhere delicious food is prepared – different countries have their own traditional dishes. Many give each other presents. If children have fasted, they are often given money by relatives and friends. Strangers and friends are all welcomed warmly to join in the feasting. No one must be alone or without food on this special day.

Many Muslims feel that for eleven months of the year they live for themselves. One month in the year they dedicate to Allah.

Ramadan helps them to create a balance in their lives, and to bring them closer to Allah. Some Muslims say they often receive important guidance for their lives during the fast. So, during Ramadan and before Eidu'l-Fitr especially, they like to thank Allah by giving the needy, as much money and food as they can.

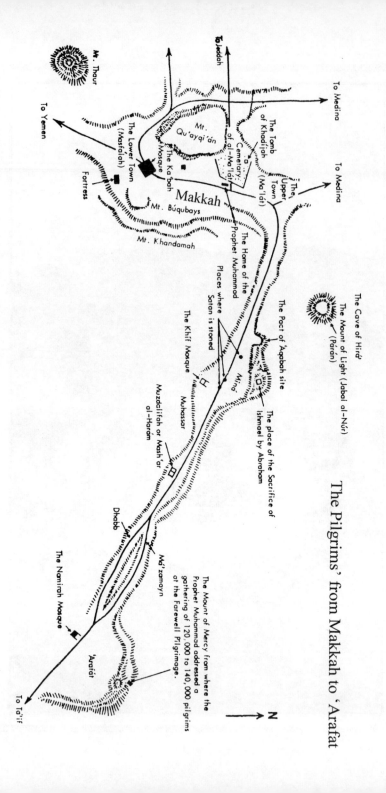

The Pilgrims' from Makkah to 'Arafāt

Mt. Thaur

To Jeddah

To Medina

To Yemen

The Lower Town
('Masfalah)

Fortress

The Ka'bah

Mt. Qu'ayqi'ān

The Tomb of Khadijah

Cemetery of al-Ma'lāt

The Mosque

Makkah

Mt. Búqubays

Mt. Khandamah

The Upper Town (Ma'lāt)

To Medina

The Home of the Prophet Muhammad

Places where Satan is stoned

The Pact of 'Aqabah site

The Cave of Hirā

The Mount of Light (Jabal al-Nūr) (Pārān)

Minā

The place of the Sacrifice of Ishmael by Abraham

The Khif Mosque

Muhassar

Muzdalifah or Mash'ar al-Harám

Dhabb

Ma'zamayn

The Namirah Mosque

'Arafāt

The Mount of Mercy from where the Prophet Muhammad addressed a gathering of 120,000 to 140,000 pilgrims at the Farewell Pilgrimage.

To Ta'if

N

Chapter 2: History of the Hajj and the Journey to Makkah

The history of the Hajj is mentioned in both the Qur'an and the Hadith. It begins at the time of Adam and Hawa (Eve) عليهما السلام. When Adam and Hawa had disobeyed Allah in Paradise, they turned in repentance to Him and He forgave them. However, He placed them on this earth not just as a punishment but because Allah, exalted is He, had always intended humans to be on earth. Here they became separated and it is said that for two hundred years they roamed the world in loneliness and sorrow, begging Allah to unite them. Finally, Allah answered their prayers and in His mercy guided Adam to the Hijaz – an area which is now part of Arabia, where the sacred city of Makkah stands.

When Adam reached this area, he understood that he had come to the centre of the world, a sacred place. The angel Jibril was sent to him to command him to lay the foundations of a sacred building. Later this building was called the Ka'bah. The angel himself placed a shining white stone – the first stone to fall to earth as a sign of the covenant between Allah and His people – in one corner of the structure. Some say that the angel Jibril had brought this stone from Heaven. The angel then taught Adam how to perform the Hajj (the Pilgrimage) and Tawaf (walking round the Ka'bah) seven times.

He took Adam to a mount in the plain of Arafat to begin performing the Hajj and it was here that Adam and Hawa met again. After two hundred years apart, perhaps they only just recognised each other, and 'Arafat which means 'recognition' is supposed to be so-named because it was there that they recognised each other. On the slopes of this mount on the Plain of 'Arafat they asked forgiveness of Allah. Then guided by the angel Jibril, they performed the Hajj.

From 'Arafat they went to the Plain of Muzdalifah where they

spent the night. Then they went to a place called Mina and after that to Makkah. At Makkah they performed the Tawaf around the Ka'bah. The names of these places appear on the map of the land we now call Arabia. But all this, of course, happened long before these places were built or had these names, and long, long before Arabia was renamed 'Saudi' Arabia!

The Ka'bah built by Adam is said to have been destroyed by the Great Flood in the time of the Prophet Nuh (Noah)~~ . All that remained was a mound.

In Islam, Adam~~ is regarded as the first prophet and the Father of all humankind.

IBRAHIM AND ISMA'IL

The Prophet Ibrahim~~ was born into a pagan society in Babylon during the reign of King Nimrod. But Allah guided Ibrahim to the Truth and he realised that it was wrong to worship idols and understood that he should only worship Allah the One. He tried to persuade his parents to do the same. But they, the inhabitants of the city and the King turned against him. They even captured him and threw him into a blazing fire to punish him for refusing to worship their gods. But Allah the Almighty protected His prophet and Ibrahim came out of the flames untouched. Life became increasingly difficult for the Prophet Ibrahim so Allah in His Mercy guided him and his wife, Sara, to emigrate first to Palestine and then to Egypt.

The King of Egypt welcomed them and they stayed there for some time. Sara was a very beautiful woman and the king asked her to be his guest at the palace because he would have liked to seduce her. However, when he attempted to seduce her three times he was prevented by a miracle, and so he let her return to Ibrahim having presented her with a woman slave called Hajirah (Hagar).

After some years, Ibrahim and Sara decided to return to Palestine. They had been married many years and were getting old, but they did not have any children. Sara suggested that Ibrahim should take her slave girl Hajirah to have children. Ibrahim~~ really wanted children and prayed to Allah to grant him his wish. Eventually his prayers were granted and Hajirah gave birth to a son, Isma'il (Ishmael). It was only some years later that Sara, who was very old by then, also gave birth to a son, Ishaq (Isaac).

IBRAHIM LEAVES HAJIRAH AND ISMA'IL IN THE BAKKAH VALLEY

In the beginning, Sara shared Ibrahim's joy at having a son, but after a little while she began to become jealous of Hajirah – perhaps because she felt that Ibrahim was taking more notice of Hajirah and her baby, than he did of her. Ibrahim was guided by Allah to take Hajirah and the young Isma'il far away to a lonely and barren place in the valley of Bakkah – this is where Makkah now stands. Ibrahim ﷺ who had total faith in the wisdom of Allah, left them sitting under a tree with just a tent, some water and dates. There were no other trees there, and no people, animals or birds. They were completely alone. As he left them Ibrahim prayed for them, saying:

"OUR LORD, I HAVE SETTLED SOME OF MY OFFSPRING... IN A VALLEY WITHOUT CULTIVATION, BY YOUR SACRED HOUSE ; IN ORDER, OUR LORD, THAT THEY MAY... (PERFORM)... REGULAR PRAYERS: SO FILL THE HEARTS OF SOME... WITH LOVE TOWARDS THEM AND FEED THEM WITH FRUITS: SO THAT THEY MAY GIVE THANKS."

(Qur'an 14: 37)

Hajirah too shared the Prophet Ibrahim's trust in Allah and accepted His Will.

The water soon ran out, and mother and child were very thirsty. Young Isma'il began crying from thirst and the intense heat. In desperation, Hajirah ran to the nearest hill called Safa, and then to another hill called Marwah, anxiously looking for water. She ran between these hills seven times becoming more and more worried. Yet she still believed that Allah would not let them die of thirst. Each time she came to the top she prayed for water.

Allah heard her prayer and where the baby Isma'il lay crying and rubbing his heels on the ground, water began to gush forth. Hajirah quickly made a ring of soil around the spring to catch the water so that they could drink from it. And she gave thanks to Allah. This spring exists today and is called the well of Zamzam. Zamzam is the Arabic word for the sound of gushing water.

For five days mother and child remained alone in that silent and desolate place. On the sixth day some people of the Jurhum tribe saw birds circling in the distance. They knew that these birds were only found where there was water, so they decided to follow them and arrived at the place where Hajirah was sitting with Isma'il. She gladly gave them her permission to settle there – after those days alone with her young son, she was pleased to have human company. But she told them that the spring would always belong to Isma'il and his descendants. A few people from another tribe also came to join them and gradually a small settlement began to grow up around the spring.

IBRAHIM DREAMS HE IS SACRIFICING ISMA'IL

One day when Ibrahim came back to visit Hajirah and Isma'il, he had a vision. In it he saw that he was sacrificing his son, Isma'il, and understood that this was a command from Allah since the visions of the prophets are true. He gently told the young Isma'il about the vision, and waited to see his reaction. Isma'il , who had total trust in the Will of Allah the Almighty, replied:

"OH MY FATHER! DO WHAT YOU ARE COMMANDED. YOU WILL FIND ME STEADFAST, IF ALLAH WILLS.

(Qur'an 37: 102)

As father and son set out to offer the sacrifice, Shaytan (Satan) tried three times to prevent them from carrying out Allah's Will but each time Ibrahim stoned Shaytan with seven pebbles to chase him away. They continued their journey and soon reached the place where they intended to perform the sacrifice.

Isma'il took off his shirt so that it would not be stained by blood, and asked his father to give it to his mother. He also asked his father to tie his hands and feet, and to sharpen the knife. He wanted to make things as easy as possible for them both. Above all, he did not want Ibrahim to feel sorry for him. Like his father, he had complete faith in Allah and believed that this was truly what Allah willed for them. As they both surrendered to Allah's Will and Ibrahim was putting his knife to Isma'il's throat, the angel Jibril put a ram there in Isma'il's place. Ibrahim heard Allah, exalted is He, saying:

"O IBRAHIM, YOU HAVE ALREADY FULFILLED THE VISION!"
(Qur'an 37: 105)

Ibrahim﮼﮿ had shown he was ready to sacrifice his son, the person that he loved most, for the love of Allah. Isma'il﮼﮿ had also shown his faith in Allah. This was the true sacrifice. Allah did not need Isma'il's flesh and blood.

THE BUILDING OF THE KA'BAH

Isma'il﮼﮿ grew up and married a girl from the Jurhum tribe. Ibrahim would visit them from time to time. It was during one of his absences, that Hajirah died.

One day the Prophet Ibrahim﮼﮿ was commanded by Allah to rebuild the House of Allah on the sacred mound where Adam had first built the Ka'bah. He asked Isma'il to help him to carry out this sacred task. So father and son worked together. Isma'il﮼﮿ carried the stones to Ibrahim who then put them in place. As the wall grew higher Isma'il gave his father a stone to stand on so that he could continue building. Ibrahim's feet left a deep mark on that stone which can still be seen near the Ka'bah at Maqam Ibrahim.

This building was in the approximate shape of a cube and because of this it was called the 'Ka'bah' which means 'cube'. Once the building had been completed, Isma'il went to look for a stone to mark the place from where pilgrims would start walking around the Ka'bah. He found the original white stone which the angel Jibril had put in the corner of the Ka'bah built by Adam, but it had grown darker due to age. It is now called al-Hajar al-Aswad or the Black Stone. This he put in the eastern corner of the building. Ibrahim was then commanded by Allah to call all the people to come and perform the Hajj. Allah told him that people:

'...WILL COME TO YOU ON FOOT AND ON EVERY KIND OF LEAN MOUNT,
COMING FROM EVERY FARAWAY POINT ON EARTH.

(Qur'an 22: 27)

He was told to proclaim the pilgrimage. Facing in each direction, in a loud voice he called the people as he had been told to do. They then performed the Hajj as Adam and Hawa had done. But now the angel Jibril instructed them to also include:

The Sa'ee' – running seven times between the two hills, Safa and Marwah, in memory of Hajirah when she was looking for water for her baby and praying for Allah's help.

The stoning of Shaytan (three rocks symbolised the Shaytan) in memory of Ibrahim chasing the Shaytan away. This was done three times.

A sacrifice at the end of the Hajj in memory of Ibrahim and Isma'il. This was also to remind people that to worship Allah it is necessary to surrender what is most dear to them.

It is interesting that the first main rite of the Hajj outside the Ka'bah is in memory of a woman's trial of faith in Allah and the strength of love for her baby son.

THE LITTLE SETTLEMENT BECOMES AN IMPORTANT CENTRE FOR TRADE

Over the centuries, the little settlement around the Zamzam spring expanded, and in time it became the City of Makkah. Its inhabitants were known as Isma'ilites because they were descendants of Isma'il . Little could be grown there as the land was barren so the people turned to trading. Gradually Makkah became an important centre for trade. Through time, nearly everyone forgot the way of Ibrahim, and some 2,500 years later, it was the task of the Prophet Muhammad to remind them and to renew their religion.

THE HAJJ

The Hajj is the biggest and most important journey in a Muslim's life. It takes place two months and two days after Ramadan. This pilgrimage is a journey of the heart and soul. It starts long before the Muslim departs from home, and careful preparations have to be made for it. These preparations can be crucial to a Muslim's experience of his or her Hajj. To receive the barakah of such a journey, it is important to prepare not only for the outer needs, but for the inner as well.

PREPARATIONS

The preparations begin from the time the decision is taken to go on Hajj. There are certain matters that must be attended to other than the travel arrangements. Debts must be repaid, and the money used for the journey should be from an honest source. Money obtained through gambling, for example, cannot be used for the pilgrimage, although there is little significance to a Hajj which is paid for from honest money if the person is not honest the rest of his life. All matters at home and work have to be left in good order. Many attend special lessons to learn about the Hajj. They also learn the special optional supplications and the meaning of all the rites they will be carrying out.

Visits are made to friends and family. Many people also visit the pilgrims before they depart. These visits are very important because when pilgrims leave for Hajj they must have made their peace with everyone, and they will go as ambassadors for their community. If a bad feeling or relationship exists between the pilgrim and another person, the pilgrim must ask that person's forgiveness. People who come to visit the pilgrims sometimes give them money to help them with their journey and they will often ask the pilgrim to remember them and pray for them when they are on the Plain of 'Arafat. This way everyone shares in the barakah or blessing of the Hajj.

When the moment of departure finally arrives, the pilgrims can leave with a light heart. They are able to go knowing they have arranged their affairs in the best way possible. As the pilgrims leave they surrender their family and friends to care of Allah.

Women who go on Hajj must have either their husband or a close male relative such as their father, brother, uncle or son to travel with them. He is there to protect them and is called their wakil, mahram or guardian.

IHRAM

All pilgrims from abroad, whether they come by boat or plane, arrive at Jeddah first. Some even walk from Africa – this can take eighteen months! On the way they pass a point near Makkah which is known as the miqat. The miqat marks the boundary of the haram – the sacred land. Before this point the pilgrim changes into ihram. A part of ihram is the complete washing of the body, and since this cannot be done in a plane, most pilgrims have done this before they set out. Ihram is a word that describes the dress of the pilgrim, as well as the state of ritual purity.

Before leaving home the pilgrims will have bathed. As their plane reaches the miqat the men put on two pieces of un-sewn, white cotton material. One piece is wrapped around the waist; the other is draped over the shoulders. Suddenly social differences between people start to disappear. A king looks exactly the same as a poor man. The university professor looks no different from the train driver. They are all just members of the same Ummah following in the footsteps of the prophets. They come from all over the world. They are black, brown, red, yellow and white, and they speak different languages. There are men and women, young and old, but they are united in their intention to undertake the Hajj in obedience to the command of Allah. Some families travel with young children and babies.

The women can wear any long dress which covers their arms and legs and wear mostly white clothes. They also cover their heads, but not their faces.

Once the pilgrims or hajjis have changed into ihram, they form their intention, and some people make a prayer in Arabic with the following words:

"O Allah, I intend to perform the Hajj, therefore make it easy for me and accept it from me."

They then start reciting the words that pilgrims recite all through the Hajj:

"Labbayka Allahumma Labbayk – Here I am at Your service O Allah, here I am at Your service!"

and will continue with words praising and glorifying Allah. They come to obey Allah's command. Now they pray that on this sacred journey, Allah will forgive them their past mistakes. They pray that Allah will bless them and their family, friends and the whole Ummah.

Being in a state of ihram means that pilgrims may not use perfume or even smell a flower. They may not quarrel or fight, nor hunt or kill animals. They will even be careful not to step on an ant. They may also not have sexual intercourse.

JOURNEY FROM JEDDAH TO MAKKAH

The old port of Jeddah with its narrow streets and carved buildings is now part of a large, modern city. It is the gateway for the pilgrims travelling to Makkah for the Hajj, who stop and rest in the Pilgrims' Village. From Jeddah the pilgrims will make their way to Makkah by bus or taxi. They might have time to do some extra shopping, but most can only think of getting to Makkah. For pilgrims arriving from cooler climates, the heat and the dryness of the air can be a shock. Depending on the time of the year, the temperature can be as high as 50°C!

MODERNISATION

In the time of the Prophet Muhammad ﷺ the journey would have been undertaken by camel. As Islam spread to distant lands the pilgrims came by sea and then camel. Their journeys sometimes took a whole year. Over the centuries this did not change very much. However, in this century travel has become cheaper and faster, so people go on Hajj in greater numbers, often travelling by plane. It became a great problem to find places for the pilgrims to stay and ways for them to travel once they arrived. In 1992, it is said that almost five million people went on Hajj.

As the Hajj is a pilgrimage to places in the Kingdom of Saudi Arabia, it is the Saudi Government who are responsible for looking after the pilgrims and the places of pilgrimage. To cope with these enormous numbers the Saudi government has modernised and expanded roads and buildings. Now there are wide motorways to speed pilgrims from one place to another. Even so, the roads can sometimes become very congested. At such times, when distances are not too great, it can be quicker to walk.

There are also many more hotels and guesthouses now. For the same reasons changes have been made to the magnificent Haram Sharif – the mosque in which the Ka'bah is located. It has been greatly enlarged and pilgrims can now pray on four floors. Despite this, when the adhan is called and people hurry to prayer, the Haram is often full and they are forced to pray in the surrounding car parks.

Chapter 3: Hajj

ARRIVAL IN MAKKAH

On arrival in Makkah the pilgrims first go to their hostel or hotel to deposit their luggage and perhaps have a short rest. After this they take wudu (ablutions) and make their way to the Haram Sharif. If it is their first time, their hearts might beat a little faster as they get the first glimpse of the Ka'bah. For those who have been on Hajj before, there is often the feeling of 'coming home'.

For most of the time during the Hajj, the pilgrims will be part of a group under the guidance of a mutawwif or if not under the direction of an experienced person who has performed the Hajj before. The mutawwif ought to know everything there is to know about the Hajj, from the prayers which can optionally be said at certain places, to the history of those places. So if pilgrims were not able to learn all the prayers – or are perhaps too overcome with emotion to remember them – the mutawwif will help them.

THE KA'BAH AND THE HARAM SHARIF

As they enter the beautiful Haram Sharif the pilgrims see the Ka'bah in the centre. It is always kept draped with a black silk cloth, with verses from the Qur'an boldly embroidered in gold thread. The cloth is called the kiswah and is changed every year. Sometimes a breeze stirs the kiswah making the cloth gently billow and ripple over the building. It almost looks as if the ancient structure is breathing.

Over the centuries, the Ka'bah has had to be repaired and rebuilt several times. However, the foundations have not been touched – they are the original stones laid by the Prophets Ibrahim and Isma'il.

At the sight of the Ka'bah – its simplicity and beauty – many find that tears start rolling down their faces, as they utter the words:

"Allah is the Most Great! Allah is the Most Great! There is no other god but Allah!"

The language of the Prophet Muhammad ﷺ was Arabic, and

so all the rites and prayers of the Hajj are also in Arabic. This is a very strong emotional and uniting factor for the pilgrims who have travelled from the distant corners of the world.

The first rite pilgrims perform is the tawaf seven times around the Ka'bah. This is done in the same direction that the earth turns and the sun moves – anticlockwise. The Black Stone, set in silver in the corner of the Ka'bah, marks the starting point of each tawaf. Traditionally, the pilgrims try and kiss it. However, because of the large number of pilgrims there, it is almost impossible for most people even to touch it. In fact, it is almost equally impossible for most people even to see it. To help pilgrims know from which point they have to begin their tawaf, a green light has been erected on the structure of the mosque opposite the Black Stone and a line in the floor extends out from the corner of the Black Stone. Before each tawaf the pilgrims greet the Stone – but they do not worship it. They can recite a different prayer before each tawaf or simply say:

"In the name of Allah; Allah the Most Great. Allah alone do we praise. Glory be to Allah!"

The prayers that are recited at each tawaf are very beautiful and moving. The following is the prayer that is traditionally recited for the seventh tawaf:

"O Allah! I ask of You perfect faith,
true conviction and a heart full of devotion towards You
a tongue busy in remembering You
vast provision, and lawful and clean earning,
sincere repentance and repentance before death,
peace at the time of death
and Your forgiveness"

As the hajjis join those already doing the Tawaf, they become swept along by the crowds. Sometimes groups of men form squares by linking arms. This is so that the women and the less strong can be protected within the squares. Here the hajjis feel as if they almost lose their own identities. They become part of the whole Ummah there, encircling the Ka'bah and praising Allah, the One. Each person might recite his own personal and individual prayer. But as the pilgrims move round the Ka'bah, they become united in this human whirlpool that never stops – day or night! As some pilgrims complete their seven tawafs and move away, others join the crowds to start their tawafs while the Ka'bah seems to float above the crowds.

MAQAM IBRAHIM

After seven tawafs the hajjis move to Maqam Ibrahim which is close by and pray there. The Maqam Ibrahim houses the stone on which the Prophet Ibrahim left his footprint. It is in the form of a beautiful gilded glass cage. Sometimes the volume of the crowds makes it impossible to pray near the Maqam Ibrahim, so the hajjis may have to pray at some distance behind it.

ZAMZAM WATER

The Tawafs can be very exhausting and after completing them the pilgrims are glad to drink water from the Zamzam well. Though the actual well is in a hall under the mosque, there are containers of the water throughout the area. The Prophet Muhammad ‎ said of this water that 'it is healing ... for whatever reason it is drunk'. When the pilgrims leave Makkah they will take containers of the Zamzam water to share with friends and relatives. But now they fill small flasks to take with them as they set off to do the next rite which is called the Sa'ee.

THE SA'EE IN REMEMBRANCE OF HAJIRAH

This rite reminds the pilgrims of Hajirah's search for water after she had been left with the young Isma'il in a barren and lonely place. The actual path between the two hills of Safa and Marwah has been covered and paved with marble. There are four 'lanes'. The two outer lanes are one-way passages in each direction for the pilgrims to walk between the two hills. The middle lanes are for those in wheelchairs. There is also another level above this laid out in the same way. At either end at ground level there are some of the original rocks left exposed where the pilgrims can rest and pray.

Sa'ee means 'to exert oneself'. To go from Safa to Marwah is one Sa'ee. The return from Marwah to Safa is another. It is necessary to complete seven Sa'ees. So the pilgrims start at Safa and finish at Marwah. The distance of each Sa'ee is about 420

metres, so all seven Sa'ees are almost three kilometres. However, there is one part in the bottom of the 'valley', today marked with green lights, over which the pilgrims move a little bit faster without running but in a sort of 'jogging' motion which is sa'ee or 'exertion'.

A FEW DAYS IN MAKKAH

During the next few days the Hajjis spend as much time as they can at the Haram Sharif. They make as many Tawafs as they feel able to and busy themselves in prayer and reading the Qur'an, as well.

This is also an opportunity to meet Muslims from other parts of the world. Because sometimes they may not have a common language, they communicate with each other through signs. They eat and pray together, and share in this experience of closeness and worship. Some people fast during the day. Although they do this for spiritual reasons, they also find that when they fast, they feel the heat less.

EIGHTH DAY OF THE MONTH OF DHI'L-HIJJAH – DAY ONE OF THE HAJJ – MINA

This is the beginning of the Hajj. All the hajjis leave Makkah and travel about seven kilometres to Mina. Here they pray at or near al-Khaif Mosque. There are so many people there that most have to pray outside. Overnight they rest in tents. At night the twinkling of the lights in the darkness seems to match the starry night sky above.

NINTH DAY OF THE MONTH OF DHI'L-HIJJAH – DAY TWO OF THE HAJJ – PLAIN OF 'ARAFAT

After the Fajr (dawn) prayers the hajjis hurry to the Plain of 'Arafat, about eight miles from Mina. The pilgrims travel by bus, although some decide to walk because of the traffic congestion or because they prefer to perform the Hajj as Muslims have done throughout history. The plain is very wide and is overlooked by the Ta'if mountains. It is a rocky desolate area that is usually quite empty and lonely. It is only at the time of the Hajj that the landscape changes as the pilgrims arrive to perform one of the most important rite of the Hajj, for as the Prophet ﷺ is reported to have said, "The Hajj is 'Arafah". In fact, this is the most important day of the Hajj. If a pilgrim does not arrive at least before the setting of the sun, his whole pilgrimage becomes invalid.

Prayers are performed in and around the Namira Mosque. A whole city of tents has been erected, with lavatories and cooking facilities. More than ever the mutawwif is important now, because if hajjis get lost in the maze of tents, they just have to give their mutawwif's name to be directed safely back to their own tent.

The day is passed in prayer. If they are strong enough, the pilgrims stand for long periods in the hot sun or in the shade of the tents making supplication. If possible they will make their way to a small mount called the Mount of Mercy. This is where Allah forgave Adam and Hawa, and also where the Prophet Muhammad ﷺ gave his Last Khutbah. Here the pilgrims can feel the reality of their insignificance before Allah, whether they are wealthy or important persons or not.

'Arafah is a time for supplication. The pilgrims join the prayer of 'Asr with the prayer of Dhuhr and then the time is purely for du'a. Facing Makkah, they pray to Allah in their own ways. Some in groups, some alone. Some outside in the searing heat, others in their tents or coaches. Eyes downcast or raised to the heavens. Hands held close to their bodies, out in front of them or stretched up to the skies. They lose themselves in prayer, repeating ayat from the Noble Qur'an or speaking to Allah with simple words which well up from their hearts. Many will sob and weep. It is said that if pilgrims pray with great sincerity in this sacred place, Allah will forgive them their wrong actions and mistakes. Anything they pray for will be granted to them. How forgetful the human being is! Allah is generous, and is present in every place and at every instant waiting to be asked. Yet, He has appointed places and times for us to ask Him, and Arafah is one of them.

As the sun sets the mood suddenly changes. The pilgrims do not prepare for the Maghrib prayer. Instead everyone starts leaving together – as the Prophet ﷺ commanded. The buses and other vehicles which crowd the road, crawl to Muzdalifah and

huge numbers walk. Muzdalifah is a plane and part of the mountain pass that stretches from 'Arafat to Makkah. However, it is not as large as the Plain of 'Arafat.

MUZDALIFAH

On arrival at Muzdalifah the hajjis first pray the Maghrib and then the 'Isha prayers. After this they all busy themselves looking for small pebbles. These will be needed the following day at Mina, and also the days after that. They need to collect forty-nine pebbles at least. Each pebble must be about the size of a chickpea or a small bean – no larger and no smaller.

Then everyone rests for a while. Some sleep in tents, others in the open air. Some prefer not to sleep at all. They leave for Mina after the Fajr prayers.

TENTH, ELEVENTH AND TWELFTH OF DHI'L-HIJJAH – EIDU'L-ADHA

Mina is not much larger than a village. So to accommodate all the pilgrims another vast tent city has been set up with many shops and services. The pilgrims stay there for three days.

STONING OF THE JAMARAT

On arrival in Mina the pilgrims go to the Jamarat or columns made out of smaller stones. There are three pillars which are symbols of shaytan. On the first day in Mina, the pilgrims throw seven stones at the larger one only. The stoning of the shaytan reminds people of the occasion when Ibrahim was on his way to sacrifice his son, and the shaytan tried to make them weaken and change their minds. After the day spent in prayer on the Plain of 'Arafat the pilgrims feel an inner peace. They feel that Allah has really forgiven them all their mistakes. When they stone the shaytan they understand that they must try to live in a better way. They must resist the shaytan and avoid doing bad things.

After this the men shave their heads, or if they are not able they trim their hair – the women just cut a small lock.

THE SACRIFICE

From Mina the pilgrims return to Makkah and perform another seven Tawafs. Muslims all over the world attend the Eidu'l-Adha prayers at their own musallas, dressing in their best clothes to celebrate the special day.

However, in Mina some of the pilgrims may have one more rite to carry out in remembrance of Ibrahim. For certain omissions and mistakes a pilgrim must offer an animal – usually a sheep or goat, in sacrifice. This is a compensation for mistakes, and the meat is shared with the needy. Animals are bought from the butchers who organise the slaughtering for the pilgrims or they may themselves slaughter their own animals. The pilgrims cook part of the meat for themselves, and give the other part to the poor. They then change out of ihram and dress in their ordinary clothes.

During the following two days celebrations continue and the pilgrims go to finish the rite of the stoning of the Jamarat. They have to throw seven stones at each of the three on both days. They also have some time to spend with fellow hajjis, friends and family, and to perhaps make even more contacts among the millions there.

After the three days in Mina they return to Makkah.

'FAREWELL TAWAF'

Once the Hajj has finished, the Hajjis usually spend some time in Makkah visiting the historical sites in the area which include the vast graveyard where some of the Prophet's companions are buried, and the cave where he received his first revelation from Allah. They also bottle as much Zamzam water as they can carry to take home with them.

When people go on Hajj they usually also visit Madinah, the city of the Prophet . If they have not been to Madinah first, they will go after completing the Hajj. But before they leave Makkah they do a last Tawaf, called the Farewell Tawaf. Some people prefer to call it the Departure Tawaf because they do not want to say "Goodbye" to Makkah forever.

Sometimes people come to Makkah to perform 'Umrah. This is a pilgrimage like the Hajj, except that people do not go to the Plain of 'Arafat nor do they celebrate Eidu'l-Adha. It can be done at any time of the year. It is a lesser pilgrimage that Muslims can perform if they want to, but it does not make them a Hajji.

Once people have completed the Hajj, they almost always want to return to Makkah again. As they gaze tearfully at the Ka'bah for the last time, the hajjis often feel that they are actually leaving their real home. A writer called Ezzedine Guellouz wrote a beautiful book called "Makkah: The Muslim Pilgrimage". In it he described his feelings:

"I was not returning from Makkah, but merely setting out."

Despite the fact that the Hajj is very exhausting, many old people try to go on the pilgrimage every year. This is because they would like to die in Makkah, because to die on Hajj is a very great blessing.

VISIT TO MADINAH

Madinah is an elegant and beautiful city – and in both appearance and atmosphere it is very different from Makkah. The streets are well laid out, and there are many shops and suqs (markets). Hajjis usually take lots of presents to everyone back home. A present from these places is always greatly valued. More than anything else visitors to this city speak of the charm, warmth and kindness of the citizens of Madinah. It is as if the feeling of brotherhood between the Muhajirun and the Ansar is still as strong as ever. Some pilgrims also tell of experiences when they have actually felt the presence of the Prophet Muhammad ﷺ.

While in Madinah the hajjis visit the Prophet's Mosque in which the Prophet's tomb is also located. Over the centuries the mosque has been enlarged, and decorated with stone carving and mosaics with a dome that opens and closes like petals of a flower. Although the building is very beautiful, the hajjis do not come just to admire it. They visit it because they want to pray in the place where their beloved Prophet ﷺ once lived, taught and worshipped. They also come to visit his tomb and greet him with the simple words:

"Peace be upon you, O Prophet, and the mercy and blessings of Allah!"

They will pray for him, his family, and his companions.

There are many places of interest in and near Madinah, and the hajjis spend time visiting some of these. Among them is the mosque built on the site of the first mosque ever built, the mosque of Quba. The hajjis come as guests of the Prophet ﷺ so they visit the places which are important in Islamic history. But nobody worships the Prophet ﷺ.

RETURN TO JEDDAH

The Hajj has been completed. Madinah has been visited. It is time to say goodbye to new friends who now feel like family. The Hajjis want to return home to see their own families, but it is hard to leave these places where the beloved Prophet ﷺ renewed the way of Islam. They leave to return home to the four corners of the earth, promising themselves that they will come back to do the Hajj again, insha'Allah (if Allah wills it). Muslims often say 'insha'Allah' when they are planning to do something, because they know that intentions and wishes will only be realised if Allah wills it.

The Hajjis travel back to Jeddah which is now overflowing with people all making their way home. In a few hours they are back on the plane or boat returning to the place from where they set off on their journeys.

RETURNING HOME

Most who have been on Hajj feel that they have changed in some way. When they return home they want to live their lives differently. They want to change their bad habits, and not think only of their own needs all the time. Many feel that they receive guidance for their lives while on Hajj. They value this deeply and want to put it into practice. When they return home they will be treated with great respect. Muslims will start to use the title 'Hajj' or 'Hajjah' in front of the pilgrims' names, for example, Hajj Rashid or Hajjah Maryam.

As the Hajjis near home, perhaps they change into festive clothes. This is a symbol of feeling renewed. They are met by family and friends who may also be beautifully dressed and who take them home to a great celebration and a feast. For the next few days – sometimes weeks – the hajjis' homes may well be full of people visiting. Everyone comes to hear about the Hajj. Each visitor might be given a tiny glass of Zamzam water or a date from Madinah, so that they can share in the barakah or blessing. Some may be fortunate enough to be given a present!

WHY THE HAJJ IS SO IMPORTANT FOR MUSLIMS

Each Hajji has a different tale to tell. Five million hajjis means five million different stories. Here is perhaps the essence of what they experience.

The pilgrims go on Hajj to obey Allah's command. They put aside all their worldly worries and come to witness and experience the sanctity of these places, and to pray because it is a special time for prayers to be answered. It is also a time during which they can devote themselves to the worship of Allah, undisturbed by the demands of daily life. They follow in the footsteps of the prophets and relive the stories of Adam and Hawa, Ibrahim, Hajirah and Isma'il. These were people who were special and important in the history of the human race. They were people who loved and worshipped Allah, and submitted to His Will. The pilgrims come to the Ka'bah to the heart of their deen – their life-transaction. They also make an inner journey – where the Ka'bah is a symbol of the heart.

Hajj is not necessarily an easy time – physically, it can be difficult to be with such enormous crowds of people and in such intense heat. Not everybody will come on Hajj with the same attitude as your own. People have different values, habits and motives, and this is inevitably reflected in their behaviour which may well be upsetting – especially as the pilgrims live in such close proximity to each other. However, these irritations are also tests and comprise part of the experience of the Hajj. It is part of learning to be tolerant towards each other and to love people for what they are, rather than what you would like them to be. Inner change is often only achieved through difficulties.

Many people say that while they are on Hajj they feel they understand the way of Islam better. They describe what their feelings were when on the Plain of 'Arafat. They see millions of Muslims like themselves, all dressed in white. Looking more closely these are people from all corners of the world: blondes with fair skins and blue eyes – perhaps from America or Western Europe; blacks – like Bilal – with the curly hair of the Africans; the brown peoples of India and Pakistan with large dark eyes; the Indonesians and Malays with almond-shaped brown eyes and black hair; the yellow skins of the Chinese; the Arabs with their distinctive noses and some of the desert Arabs with a distinctive chocolate brown which is seen nowhere else on earth. All shapes and sizes. All ages. Men, women and children. All kinds of backgrounds. There are doctors, lawyers, shopkeepers, shepherds, teachers, singers, experts on the Qur'an, those who know little of the Qur'an... everyone here is different. But they all have the opportunity to feel united at this time with one purpose – to worship Allah together, to experience the benefit of praying as one community. For someone who is really sincere in his devotion, this will surely be his experience.

For the first time the pilgrims will feel what it is to be truly a member of the whole human race – not just of their own country, town or village. They begin to understand that to be Muslim is something much greater than to be just an Arab, an Indian, an Iranian, an Englishman or an Indonesian. They feel the strength of the Ummah that the Prophet ﷺ first created in Madinah, now a world Ummah.

Hajjis often talk about amazing meetings that they have had with complete strangers. They speak of fascinating conversations. These meetings are also an important part of their experiences as are the physical difficulties that they encounter on this journey.

Apart from coming on Hajj to obey Allah's command, the pilgrims also come because they need to pray. They pray for all sorts of things. They pray for themselves and their families. For their friends. For the whole Ummah of Islam. They pray for forgiveness, for peace, for health and perhaps enough money to live without worries. They pray for the Prophet Muhammad ﷺ and his Companions – the first Muslims, and also the other prophets.

The biggest experience for most pilgrims is the tawaf – and then later, standing and praying on the Plain of 'Arafat. Performing the tawafs, swept along by the crowds all moving round the Ka'bah, the pilgrims begin to feel a freedom. Everything that before stopped them from showing their feelings disappears.

It is as if they are being 'unwound'. It seems that they are there with the whole human race going round and round and round. Yet in the constant movement, they feel a calm place inside themselves, and they feel close to Allah.

They have probably never felt so close to Allah before. This helps them to open their hearts to Allah and pray. Later, on the Plain of 'Arafat, when they pray with tears streaming down their faces, as they focus on their lives and their needs they ask Allah's forgiveness. Here there is almost no movement of the crowds in the burning sun, despite the enormous number of people. In this place they find that they can talk to Allah. There are no barriers. They know – they can really feel – that Allah hears them, that Allah forgives them their wrong actions and mistakes as He forgave Adam and Hawa and that Allah will answer their prayers as He promised Adam and Hawa.

Most of the pilgrims feel that during the Hajj, they have gone through a deep change. A change that will affect their whole life. They have developed a deeper understanding of their way and what it means to be a Muslim. They feel they have been given a second chance and that they have been reborn.

Months of the Muslim Calendar

WITH DATES OF MAIN HISTORICAL EVENTS

MUHARRAM

1 – Muslim New Year
10 – Yawm 'Ashura

SAFAR

27 – Start of Hijrah. Date Prophet Muhammad ﷺ left Makkah for Yathrib (Madinah)

RABI' AL-AWWAL

9 – Muhammad ﷺ was appointed by Allah to become a Prophet to renew and spread Islam
12 – Milad un-Nabi – The Prophet's Birthday ﷺ

RABI' AL-THANI

JUMADA'L-ULA

JUMADA 'TH-THANI

RAJAB

27 – Mi'raj an-Nabi – Prophet Muhammad's Ascension ﷺ

SHA'BAN

14 – Lailat al-Bara'at – Night of Destiny when each person's fate is decided for the following year. Muslims pray on this night that a bad fate may be removed from them and that Allah may grant them a good year. Although it is not mentioned in the Qur'an, some say that the Prophet ﷺ used to celebrate this night.

RAMADAN

1 – The Fast begins
17 – Battle of Badr
18 – Conquest of Makkah

SHAWWAL

1 – Eidu'l- Fitr. The end of the Ramadan Fast.
6 – Battle of Uhud
26 – Journey of Ta'if – After the death of his uncle, Abu Talib, the Prophet ﷺ and his followers suffered persecution. The Prophet ﷺ went to a town called Ta'if, to see whether the citizens of Ta'if would allow the Muslims to move there. However the Prophet ﷺ was greeted with great hostility. Later the Muslims emigrated to Yathrib (Madinah).

DHU'L-QA'DAH

DHU'L-HIJJAH

9 – Yawm al-'Arafat – The Hajj
10 – Eidu'l-Adha

Glossary

Ayah	Verse of the Qur'an.
Ablutions	To wash oneself in a special way before praying or reading the Qur'an.
Adab	Courtesy, good manners and respect for others.
A'ishah	One of the Prophet Muhammad's wives. She ﴾﴿ was the daughter of Abu Bakr ﴾﴿ and married the Prophet ﷺ when she was very young. Born about 613 CE. Died 678 CE. She was a very intelligent woman and after the Prophet's death people used to come to her to settle questions on Islam. Much of what is contained in the Hadith literature also came from her. She was the only woman who had not been previously married when she became the Prophet's wife.
Ibrahim	Arabic/Muslim name for the Prophet Abraham ﴾﴿ .
Adhan	The Muslim call to prayer.
Akhirah	The Hereafter. Life after death. All Muslims believe in the Akhirah. Each person's actions in this world are recorded by angels. When we die Allah will judge us on these. People who have had a true tawhid, worshipped Allah and done good deeds will be rewarded with the joys of the Garden. Those who have associated

others with Allah, turned away from Allah and done bad things, will be punished
in the burning fires of Hell. It is also well
to remember that Allah may forgive the
people of tawhid who had serious wrong
actions, and punish the people of shirk
who had good actions.

Allah

The Arabic divine name. Both Arab Christians and Muslims use this name.

Ansar

'Helpers'. They were the Muslims of Madinah who helped and supported the
Prophet ﷺ and the Makkan Muslims
when they emigrated to Madinah from
Makkah.

Arkanu'l-Islam

The five 'Pillars of Islam' which are the
most important things that every Muslim
has to do. See section 'Some Things that
Make a person a Muslim'.

al-Asma al-Husna

The ninety-nine beautiful names of Allah.
In the Qur'an there are many descriptions
of Allah's qualities, like Allah the Merciful, the All-Powerful, the Creator, the All-
Knowing. Muslims praise Allah by reciting these names. See Dhikr.

'Asr

The name given to the prayers that are
performed in the middle of the afternoon.

As-salamu 'alaikum

Muslim greeting: "May the Peace and
Blessings of Allah be upon you!" This is
said when Muslims meet and part. It is
also used in the family when they see each
other first thing in the morning, or before
they go to bed at night. If someone greets

you with these words, you should reply:
Wa 'alaikum as-salam! – "And on you, be
peace!"

Barakah	Blessing or Grace of Allah.
Bakkah Valley	Valley in Arabia where Makkah is situated
Beneficent	Good, generous, kind. However, it is difficult to find an accurate translation of the Arabic word, ar-Rahman. Shems Friedlander in his book "Ninety-Nine Names of Allah" gives the following description: "He Who gives blessings and prosperity to all beings..."
Bilal	An Abyssinian slave who became an early convert to Islam. He was the first man to call the adhan (the call to prayer). A man who calls the adhan is called a 'mu'adh-dhin' or sometimes a 'bilal'.
Black Stone	The stone, which is said to be a meteorite, placed in an outside corner of the Ka'bah which marks the place where the tawaf should begin.
Blood Money	Compensation paid to a relative or tribe for a person's death. This was often used to prevent revenge killings.
Buraq	A mystical, shining animal with wings. It looked a bit like a cross between donkey and a mule. Each of its strides was so wide that it reached the horizon. It appeared with the Angel Jibril to carry the Prophet Muhammad ﷺ to Jerusalem. See Isra' and Mi'raj.

Caliph	Head of the Ummah or the Muslim community. After the Prophet Muhammad's death, Abu Bakr﷐ was appointed the first Caliph. Also written Khalifah following the Arabic spelling.
Caravan	A group of traders or other travellers making a journey for trade, which travelled across the desert with a train of camels.
Deen	Deen is often wrongly translated as 'religion' but religion has come to mean only belief in God and Angels, etc., and acts of worship. For this reason deen is increasingly translated as 'life-transaction' a term encompassing also trade, commerce, marriage, divorce, and all the other affairs of living, since the revelation has guidance on all life.
Dhikr	A way of worshipping and praising Allah by repeating certain words like Allahu Akbar "Allah is the Most Great" or Laa ilaha illa'llah "There is no god but Allah". Sometimes a Muslim uses a 'tasbih' (beads) to keep track of the number of times he repeats a prayer.
Dhuhr	Name given to the prayers that are performed just after noon.
Dunya	The world. Also life in this world.
Eid	'Recurring happiness' or 'festivity'. It is used for the two major Muslim festivals, Eidu'l-Fitr and Eidu'l-Adha. Eidu'l-Fitr is celebrated after the Fast of Ramadan. Eidu'l-Adha takes place during the Hajj

(Pilgrimage) and celebrates the story of Ibrahim and his son, Isma'il, when Ibrahim was asked by Allah to sacrifice his son.

Fajr

Dawn. Also the name of the prayers performed at dawn.

Fast, to fast

A Muslim fast is when a person does not eat or drink anything during the hours of daylight, for one or any number of days. The Fast is usually the fast done during the month of Ramadan. There are also other fasts that a Muslim can do if he wants.

Fatihah

Surah al-Fatihah or 'The Opening'. The first chapter of the Qur'an. It is the chapter that is recited most frequently and forms part of the daily prayers. It is said to be the essence of the whole Qur'an.

Fatimah

Youngest daughter of the Prophet Muhammad ﷺ and Khadijah. She married Ali, the Prophet's cousin. She was known for her devotion to the Prophet ﷺ and also because she was a very spiritual and pure woman. She died five month's after her father's death ﺭﺿﻰ ﺍﻟﻠﻪ ﻋﻨﻬﺎ .

Gregorian Calendar

In 1582 Pope Gregory XIII introduced a calendar which was based on a previous calendar called the Julian Calendar. It has 365 days in the year with an extra day each leap year. The calendar was named after Pope Gregory and is the one used all over the world today. It was a reform of the existing Roman solar calendar – the Romans worshipped the Sun.

Hadith	Collection of the sayings and advice of the Prophet Muhammad ﷺ.
Hafidh	A person who can recite the whole Qur'an by heart.
Hajj	The Pilgrimage to Makkah that every Muslim should try to undertake – if he or she can afford.
Hajji	A Muslim who has completed the Hajj or the Pilgrimage. More often called Hajj (pronounced Haajj) or in the case of a woman Hajjah.
Hajirah	Arabic/Muslim name for Hagar. She was a woman slave who was given to Sara by the King of Egypt. Sara gave her to Ibrahim ﷺ and she gave birth to his son Isma'il/Ishmael ﷺ.
Halal	Those things that are permitted to a Muslim. Opposite of haram. This word can be used for food, drink, actions or behaviour.
Halimah	The Prophet Muhammad's wet-nurse. See wet-nurse.
Haram	Those things which are forbidden to a Muslim. Opposite of Halal. This word can be used for food, drink, actions or behaviour.
Haram Sharif	The great mosque in Makkah which contains the Ka'bah.
Hawa	Arabic/Muslim name for Eve, Adam's wife.

Hijrah	The emigration of Muslims from Makkah to Madinah in 622 CE. The Makkan Muslims left their homes because they were being persecuted by the Quraysh.
'Ibadah	'Worship' from the same root as 'abd – slave. Thus service is also worship.
Iftar	The Breaking of the Fast.
Ihram	The clothes a pilgrim wears when he goes on Hajj. The men wear two pieces of unsewn white cotton cloth. One piece is wrapped around the waist. The other is worn over the shoulders. The women wear long dresses which cover their bodies completely except for their hands and faces. They also have to cover their heads. To be in Ihram also means to obey the rules of purity which are part of the Hajj. See section on Hajj
Imam	Leader of the Muslims. Formerly used for the Khalifah or the Amir, now used almost exclusively for the leader of prayers in the mosque. There are no priests in Islam. An Imam is also often a leader of the community. The man who is chosen to be an Imam is usually the person who knows the din of Islam the best. But above all he will be well-loved and respected by the community. In the early days of Islam a young boy once became the Imam because he was able to recite the Qur'an better than anybody else in his tribe. He was so poor he did not even have any clothes. The rest of the tribe had to find something for him to wear to cover up his

nakedness so that he could lead the prayers!

Iman	Faith. The word means to 'affirm', 'to trust', 'to believe' or 'to know', 'to be so sure that there is not even a little bit of doubt' (in a person's faith and trust in Allah).
Insha'Allah	This means 'Allah willing'. When a Muslim says he is going to do something, he often adds the words: 'insha'Allah'. He knows that what he wants to do will only be successful if Allah wills it.
'Isa	Arabic/Muslim name for the Prophet Jesus. In the Qur'an, 'Isa ﷽ is spoken of as a very devoted person. However, he is not the son of Allah. The nature of Allah is such that he does not have any parents, children or partners, for the son of a god would be a god, and one universe could not have two gods.
'Isha	The name given to the prayers which are performed at night.
Isma'il	Ishmael ﷽ . Son of Ibrahim and Hajirah.
Islam	Islam (pronounced Islaam) means 'submission to the commands and prohibitions of Allah and of His Messenger' and it derives from a root from which also salam 'Peace' derives.
Isra'	The journey the Prophet Muhammad ﷺ made with the angel Jibril to the Mosque in Jerusalem. He made the journey rid-

ing on an animal called the Buraq. See section on 'Isra'.

Jama'ah

Congregation. The people who perform prayers together, usually at a mosque.

Jamarat

The stone pillars which are the symbol of Shaytan. These are stoned during the Hajj in memory of when the Prophet Ibrahim حسنه chased away Shaytan because Shaytan tried to prevent him from obeying Allah by sacrificing Isma'il.

Jibril

Arabic/Muslim name for the angel Gabriel.

Jihad

'Struggle' or 'striving' for the sake of Allah. This can be to fight to make the word of Allah and His shari'ah uppermost in the earth and to protect one's deen or one's freedom. It also means to fight for the weak, and to fight against what is bad. The Prophet ﷺ called this 'the lesser Jihad'. 'The greater Jihad' is fighting the bad in ourselves.

Jumu'ah

Friday congregational prayers. Prayers that are held every Friday that Muslim men must attend. Women do not have to go, although they may if they want.

Jurhum Tribe

The tribe that settled near the well of Zamzam when Hajirah and Isma'il were left alone in the Bakkah Valley.

Kafir

Somebody who 'covers' over the truth, or is 'ungrateful' to Allah and His Messenger. Its meaning is much wider than the idea of someone who does not believe in Allah. The People of the Book who do believe in God but do not believe in the Messenger of Allah ﷺ and in some of the other Prophets are also kafirun.

Ka'bah	Ka'bah means 'cube'. It is the name of the House of Allah in Makkah which is the central point of the Hajj or Pilgrimage. See section on the History of the Hajj.
Khadijah	A very successful business women and a noble member of the Quraysh tribe. She became the Prophet Muhammad's first wife. She bore him six children including Fatimah. Their two sons died when very young.
Khutbah	A discourse delivered on the Jumu'ah or at the Eid prayers. It contains remembrance and praise of Allah, exhortation to follow the right way, admonition, blessings on the Prophet ﷺ and supplication.
Kiswah	Silken black cloth with ayat from the Noble Qur'an embroidered on it with gold thread which covers the Ka'bah.
Lunar Month	The lunar month is 29 or 30 days long. It is counted from the time there is a new moon. The next new moon marks the beginning of the next month.
Lunar Calendar	The lunar calendar consists of 12 lunar months and is 10 days shorter (11 days in a leap year) than the calendar used in the West called the Gregorian Calendar.

Maghrib	The prayers that are performed right after sunset.
Mahram	Wakil/guardian. If a woman wants to go on Hajj she must be accompanied by her husband or a male member of her family who will be her guardian.
Maryam	Arabic/Muslim name for Mary, mother of the Prophet 'Isa﴿عليه السلام﴾. In the Noble Qur'an it is said that Allah raised her spiritually above all other women of her time. It also tells of how she conceived the baby 'Isa without having contact with any man. She was known for her purity.
Marwah	One of the hills in Makkah that Hajirah ran up looking for water for her young son, Isma'il. The other hill was called Safa.
Mutawwif	A guide used during the Hajj. He can guide the pilgrims and tell them what prayers they have to say, where they have to go, and also help them with other things. They usually know a lot about the history of the Hajj.
Miqat	The boundary line which marks where the haram of the Makkan area begins. This goes back to before the time of the Prophet Muhammad ﷺ. When the Muslims returned to Makkah and the temples were purified, the Prophet ﷺ marked out this area again.
Masjid	Arabic word for Mosque. See Mosque.
Mimbar	The steps in a mosque where the Imam stands when he gives the khutbah.

Mi'raj

The Prophet Muhammad's ascension during which he visited the seven heavens and rose above them to the presence of Allah, exalted is He, where he approached closer than any other human before or since.

Monotheist

A person who believes in Allah, the One. However, Tawhid is often translated incorrectly as monotheism which is thought of by the Jews and Christians as merely signifying belief in one god. Tawhid rather means to realise that everything that comes to you, whether good or bad, comes from Allah alone.

Mosque

A masjid. A place where Muslims congregate for prayer. Women are permitted to pray in the mosque and usually do so at the rear. It will also have toilets and places for washing and taking Wudu – separate for men and women. A larger mosque usually has a minaret, i.e. a tall tower from which the adhan (call to prayer) is called. The Companions, however, used to call the prayer from the door of the Mosque. Since the Mosque is the centre for the entire civilisation of Islam, it is usually accompanied by other structures which are best exemplified by the complexes built by the Ottomans called 'Imarets'. An Imaret comprised a mosque, a madrasah (school), clinic and hospital, a market open to everyone without any rent being charged for it, a caravanserai which was a hostel to look after travellers, and often a soup kitchen where the poor were fed.

Larger mosques are usually built with at least one dome, a minaret and a large square or courtyard.

Mu'min	A person who affirms and believes in Allah, His Messengers, His Books, His Angels, the Last Day and that the Decree, both and the good and the evil of it is from Allah, exalted is He. Someone who has Iman or complete trust in Allah.
Musa	Arabic/Muslim name for the Prophet Moses ﵇.
Musalla	The place outside a city or town where the Muslims perform the Eid prayer. A city may have a number of jumu'ah mosques but for the Eid prayers all the people of the city gather at the one place.
Musallah	Prayer mat.
Nuh	Arabic/Muslim name for the Prophet Noah ﵇.
Oasis	(Plural: oases). A fertile area in the desert where there is water. An oasis is a green, fertile area in the middle of the desert, with lots of trees – usually palm or date trees. There are often settlements there, and sometimes, if there is enough water, there are even farms. Oases were very important at the time that the Prophet Muhammad ﷺ lived because caravans could stop there to rest and stock up with food and water on their long journeys across the desert. In those days journeys took a very long time.

Qiblah	The direction of the Ka'bah, towards which Muslims face when they pray
Quraysh	The most powerful tribe in Makkah at the time of the Prophet Muhammad ﷺ and the tribe to which he belonged.
Qur'an	The speech of Allah revealed to the Messenger of Allah, Muhammad ﷺ. It is in the form of many powerful and beautiful ayat. See section on the Qur'an.
Ramadan	The month of the Muslim calendar during which Muslims must fast from dawn to dusk each day.
Revelation	To 'reveal' means to show something that was hidden before. Allah revealed to the Prophet Muhammad ﷺ things that he did not know before. These usually took the form of guidance for the Prophet ﷺ personally, or to help him with his mission, and for the Muslim community until the end of time. Allah, exalted is He, also addresses the Jews, the Children of Isra'il, the Christians, the People of the Book and all of mankind in this Glorious Qur'an.
Sadaqah	Commonly today it is thought of as something which is given from one's own free will to someone in need and that it is different from Zakat. However, in the original meaning sadaqah and zakah mean the same thing, i.e. the obligatory portion taken by the Amir or his appointed collectors from wealth which amounts to the measure known as the nisab and which has been held untouched for a year. The

Amir then distributes it among the eight categories who merit it. Sadaqah has come to mean personal generosity which can be in almost any form, for example, food, clothes or money. Even helping someone to do or learn something, cheering up somebody who is sad, or comforting them, can be called sadaqah.

Sa'ee

Sa'ee means to exert oneself. On Hajj it is the name given to the passing seven times between the two hills of Safa' and Marwah (seven Sa'ees). Hajirah did this when she was looking for water for the young Isma'il. During the Hajj, pilgrims perform this rite in remembrance of Hajirah's desperation and faith, and of how Allah answered her prayer.

Safa

One of the hills in Makkah that Hajirah ran up looking for water for her young son, Isma'il. The other hill was called Marwah.

Sahabah

The Companions of the Prophet Muhammad.

Suhur

The breakfast that Muslims eat before they start fasting during Ramadan.

Salah

The prayers that Muslims perform five times each day.

Salman

A Persian slave who became a Muslim. The Prophet ﷺ helped him buy his freedom. He gave the Prophet ﷺ the idea to dig a trench around the exposed part of Madinah to protect the Muslims from the attack of the Makkan army. Because this technique was used the battle is known as 'The Battle of the Trench'.

Sara

Arabic/Muslim name for Sarah, the Prophet Ibrahim/Abraham's first wife.

ﷺ

This, or s.a.w., (PBUH) or (SAAS) is often seen after the name of the Prophet Muhammad. Whenever Muslims mention the Prophet's name, they usually say: s.a.w. – salla'llahu alaihi wa sallam – May the Peace and Blessings of Allah be upon him. Similarly, they pray for a Prophet by saying 'alaihi's-salam – Peace be upon him, or one of the Companions by saying radiya'llahu 'anhu – may Allah be pleased with him.

Shahadah

The Muslim creed: Laa ilaha illa'llah Muhammadur-rasulu'llah which means: There is no god but Allah, and Muhammad is the Messenger of Allah.

Shaytan

Arabic/Muslim name for Satan. The Devil. He is not a powerful evil force as in popular Christian imaginings but a whisperer who insinuates thoughts into people's breasts to lead them astray. He has only the power that the slave allows him.

Suq

A market.

Sunnah

The customary behaviour of the Prophet Muhammad ﷺ and also of the Caliphs who took the right way after him. The Sunnah is the embodiment of the revelation of the Qur'an.

Tasbih	Muslim beads. They usually consist of ninety-nine beads completed by an extra piece, called an alif, to make a hundred, or eleven beads, or thirty three beads divided by larger beads into groups of eleven.
Wakil	A guardian.
Wet-nurse	A woman who breast-feeds someone else's baby. Sometimes it is because the mother is not able to. In this story however, the climate in Makkah was considered unhealthy so the Prophet's mother wanted her baby to be brought up for those first vital years in a healthier place.
Wudu	The way of washing before performing the prayers. First the hands are washed; then the mouth, nose and face. After this the arms and hands are washed up to the elbows, then the hair is wiped over with wet hands and the ears are washed. Finally the feet are washed up to the ankles. Each part is washed three times, apart from the head and the ears, always beginning with the right side.
Ya'qub	Arabic/Muslim name for the Prophet Jacob who is also known as Isra'il﴿ﷺ﴾ .
Yusuf	Arabic/Muslim name for the Prophet Joseph.
Zakat	A 'poor-tax'. The obligatory portion taken by the Amir or his appointed collectors from wealth which amounts to the measure known as the nisab and which has

been held untouched for a year. The Amir then distributes it among the eight categories who merit it, who include the poor and needy, those indebted, to free slaves, in the way of Allah (for jihad), and for travellers, etc.

Zakat al-Fitr

A special zakah consisting of foodstuffs such as grains, pulses, and dates, etc., collected during Ramadan to help the poor and needy celebrate the Eid.

Zamzam

The well that sprang up when Hajirah was looking for water for Isma'il in the Bakkah Valley. This water is said to be pure and has very special healing powers. Pilgrims always take some home with them to share with family and friends. Over the centuries before Islam, the spring became buried. It was Abd al-Muttalib, the Prophet Muhammad's grandfather, who rediscovered it and removed the earth and stones from it.

Sources

THE HOLY QUR'AN, Text, Translation & Commentary by Ali, A. Yusuf, Beirut, Dar al Arabia, 1968

THE MESSAGE OF THE QUR'AN, Translated & Explained by Asad, Muhammad, Gibraltar, Dar al-Andalus, 1980

THE GLORIOUS QUR'AN, Translation of, by Zidan, Dr. Ahmad & Zidan, Mrs. Dina, 1991

AN-NAWAWI'S FORTY HADITH, Damascus, The Holy Koran Publishing House, 1976

Aziz, Qutubuddin: THE PROPHET AND THE ISLAMIC STATE, Karachi, Islamic Media Corporation, 1990

CONVERSATIONS WITH HAJJIS including Hajji Muhammad Ridhwan Is'harc

Dinet, E. & ben Ibrahim, Sliman: THE LIFE OF MOHAMMAD, The Prophet of Allah, Karachi, Taj Company Ltd.

Draper, John William: A HISTORY OF THE INTELLECTUAL DEVELOPMENT OF EUROPE, London, 1875, Vol. I, p. 329

Esin, Emil: MECCA THE BLESSED, MADINAH THE RADIANT, London, Elek Books, 1963

Ezzedine, Gouelouz: Mecca, THE MUSLIM PILGRIMAGE, Translation of PELERINAGE A LA MECQUE, New York and London, Paddington Press, 1979

Friedlander, Shems with al-Hajj Shaikh Muzaffereddin: NINETY-NINE NAMES OF ALLAH, San Francisco, Harper, San Francisco, 1993

Hamid, AbdulWahid: ISLAM, THE NATURAL WAY, London, MELS, 1989

Halim, Mrs. H. of Iqra Trust, London: TEACHING MATERIALS ON THE HAJJ – 1993

Hart, Michael H: THE 100 – A RANKING OF THE MOST INFLUENTIAL PERSONS IN HISTORY, New York, 1978

Ibn Ishaq: THE LIFE OF MUHAMMAD, APOSTLE OF ALLAH, (edited by Michael Edwarde), London, The Folio Society, 1964

Kandhalvi, Shaikul Hadith Maulana Muhammad Zahariyya: FAZAIL-E-AMAL, THE TEACHINGS OF ISLAM – Stories of Sahabah, Translated by Arshad, Abul Rashid, New Delhi, Idara Ishaat-e-Diniyat, 1983

Karim, Al-Haj Maulana Fazlul, MA BL: English Translation and

Commentary of Al-Hadis of Mɪsʜκaτ-υʟ-Masaʙɪʜ, Dacca, Published by Author, 1960

Khan, Dr. Muhammad Muhsin of Al Madinah Al Munauwara, Islamic University: Tʀaɴsʟaτɪoɴ oϝ τʜe Meaɴɪɴɢs oϝ Saʜɪʜ Aʟ Bυκʜaʀɪ, – Gujranwala Cantt. West Pakistan, Taleem-ul-Qur'an Trust, 1971

Lings, Martin: Mυʜammad; ʜɪs ʟɪϝe ʙased oɴ τʜe eaʀʟɪesτ soυʀces, Cambridge, UK, The Islamic Texts Society, 1991

Nadwi, S Abul Hasan Ali: Maɴκɪɴd's Deʙτ τo τʜe Pʀoʜeτ Mυʜam-mad, Oxford Centre for Islamic Studies, Oxford, 1989

Najaar, Sheikh Abubaker, 77 Seʟecτed Sτoʀɪes ϝʀom τʜe Qυʀ'aɴ, Cape, South Africa, 1992

Qazi, M A: A Coɴcɪse Dɪcτɪoɴaʀʏ oϝ ISLAMIC TERMS, Noor Publishing House, Delhi , 1989

Rahman, Afzular: Roʟe oϝ Mυsʟɪm Womeɴ ɪɴ Socɪeτʏ, London, Seerah Foundation, 1986

Toynbee, Arnold J: Cɪvɪʟɪzaτɪoɴ oɴ Tʀɪaʟ, New York, 1948, p. 28